Finding God in The Lord of the Rings

Finding GOD in THE LORD OF THE RINGS

KURT BRUNER
JIM WARE

TYNDALE HOUSE PUBLISHERS, INC.
WHEATON, ILLINOIS

Visit Tyndale's exciting Web site at www.tyndale.com

First printing of Living Books edition October 2003.

Living Books is a registered trademark of Tyndale House Publishers, Inc.

Edited by Lisa A. Jackson

Designed by Jenny Swanson

ISBN 0-8423-8555-X

Printed in the United States of America

07 06 05 04 03
5   4   3   2   1

To all who search for light in Middle-earth:

Eala Earendel engla beorhtast
Ofer Middangeard monnum sended.

(Hail Earendel, brightest of angels
Sent to men over Middle-earth)

TABLE OF
CONTENTS

INTRODUCTION

On a drizzly day in October 1999 I realized a life dream: to visit a little pub in a remote corner of Oxford called The Eagle and Child. I didn't want a drink. What I wanted was a photograph of me sitting where two of my literary heroes had routinely gathered half a century earlier.

In London for a *Focus on the Family Radio Theatre* recording session, I carved out a day and headed to Oxford in order to locate the pub. I expected it to be more obvious. (In the United States there would be an entire tourist attraction built around it.) By the looks of the place, you'd never know that it had been frequented by such famous writers as C. S. Lewis and J. R. R. Tolkien. I found no sign marking the table they had graced while critiquing one another's work. Apparently, it was no big deal to the present management—which was more interested in whether or not I was buying a drink. But it was quite a big deal to me. I was standing in the very pub where the writing group called The Inklings had met during the days when such classics as *The Chronicles of Narnia* and *The Lord of the Rings* were taking form! Some people visit Graceland to celebrate the memory of Elvis. I went to Oxford to celebrate two Christian men whose writings have impacted the faith and imaginations of millions.

J. R. R. Tolkien, who helped C. S. Lewis on his journey to Christian faith, wrote *The Lord of the Rings,* the epic fantasy that became the most popular book of the twentieth century. It sold more than fifty million copies and inspired the film trilogy from New Line Cinema. People of all faiths have enjoyed the adventures of Frodo, Sam, Gandalf, and others on a quest to save the Shire from impending doom—and with good reason. The craft and creativity behind this wonderful fantasy rank it among the greatest literary works of all time. But many Tolkien fans may not realize that it was a strong Christian faith that inspired and informed the writer's imagination. In fact, many hard-line believers have been hesitant to embrace a creative work that includes mythic figures, magic rings, and supernatural themes. This is unfortunate because the transcendent truths of Christianity bubble up throughout this story, baptizing our imaginations with realities better experienced than studied. Like the works of C. S. Lewis, Tolkien's myth and fantasy can open the heart's back door when the front door is locked. As he explained, "I believe that legends and myths are largely made of 'truth,' and indeed present aspects of it that can only be received in this mode."[1] The result has been that millions, many of whom reject formal religion, have encountered realities that flourish in the unexplored regions of Christian belief.

FICTIONAL REALITIES

The *Lord of the Rings* adventure takes place in the fantastic world of Middle-earth, a land given birth and form in J. R. R. Tolkien's imagination. It is an ancient world thriving with men, elves, dwarves, and hobbits who live in relative harmony while enjoying the blessings of peace and prosperity. Like us, they know the joys and duties of life in any era: hard work, growing children, curious neighbors, and festive celebrations.

The hobbits and other inhabitants of Middle-earth have a rich heritage of songs, ballads, legends, and folklore that infuse otherwise mundane lives with meaning. Some of the songs tell the tale of an evil ruler named Sauron and his dark tower in the ancient land of Mordor. But there are more happy legends of noble warriors and the council of the wise who freed the world from darkness to establish a land of peace and goodness. Whether the stories are history or myth is little contemplated among the hobbits as they go about their busy routines. More recent stories have taken center stage and become bigger-than-life, such as how Bilbo Baggins obtained long life and great wealth. The friendly, simple hobbit had been part of a risk-filled adventure many years earlier, including the time he found a magic ring during his famous encounter with the despicable Gollum. His full story is told in another classic, *The Hobbit*.

One of the most charming aspects of Tolkien's mythic realm is that, though clearly fictional, it has the feel of a time and region that were once real, possibly long forgotten parts of our own ancient history. This is no accident. Its creator went to great lengths to shape a fantasy world that consistently reflects those realities that frame the story in which men of all ages have lived. As a Christian, Tolkien understood that our lives are part of a grand drama that both transcends and explains our experiences. The drama's narrative infuses meaning into scenes and events that would otherwise seem arbitrary and meaningless. Tolkien saw the adventure of our lives, like the adventure of his hobbits, as part of a story that began "once upon a time" and is moving toward its eventual "ever after."

Tolkien's elves, dwarves, hobbits, and other mythic personalities become real as we identify with their fears and failures, sorrows and successes. Their story is our story: a compelling picture of the epic drama playing out on the stage of time and eternity. So many aspects of Tolkien's world mirror the fabric of our own.

For example, the characters recognize that they are part of a story being told.

"What a tale we have been in, Mr. Frodo, haven't we?" reflects Sam after surviving one of many dangerous encounters. Throughout their adventure Frodo and Sam openly discuss the fact that they are in a story, recognizing that the scenes of life are not random or purposeless, but key events in the great drama in which we play a part. Their outlook reflects the Christian understanding of providence, that we are all part of a story being written by the creator of all that is.

Middle-earth is in its third age, so it is a world with history. Throughout the book, characters recite poems and songs that tell the tales of ancient past, acknowledging that there is a story behind their story. Careful to pass the stories from one generation to the next, they recognize that what has been gives meaning and context for what is.

Tolkien's fantasy world, like our real world, is one in which good seeks to protect and preserve while evil seeks to dominate and destroy. His characters know that behind the increasingly dark cloud of oppression lurks one who seeks vengeance for past humiliation. In several chilling scenes, the evil Sauron is described as displaying many diabolical characteristics that seem to reflect those of the biblical Satan.

The Lord of the Rings is a tale of redemption in which the main characters overcome cowardly self-preservation to model heroic self-sacrifice. Their bravery mirrors the greatest heroic rescue of all time, when Christ "humbled himself and became obedient to death—even death on a cross!" (Philippians 2:8).

These and other themes of Tolkien's fictional story reflect what we know to be the ultimate true story. In Tolkien's words, "The Gospels contain a fairy-story, or a story of a larger kind which embraces all the essence of fairy-stories. They contain many marvels, particularly artistic, beautiful, and moving: 'mythical' in their perfect, self-contained significance. . . . But this story has entered History and the primary world. . . . This story is supreme; and it is true. Art has been verified. God is the Lord, of angels, and of men—and of elves."[2] It is this understanding of reality that makes *The Lord of the Rings* one of the greatest fantasies of all time.

We wrote this book to help fans of *The Lord of the Rings* discover how the rich fabric of Tolkien's fantasy world enhances a Christian understanding of our real world. Each reflection begins with a scene or theme of the adventure that points to a truth or insight for our lives today. We are assuming that the reader is familiar with the entire trilogy, as the concepts explored are intended to enrich the experience of the full story, not replace it.

We do not claim to know the mind of J. R. R. Tolkien beyond what he chose to share with us through letters and other writings. It is unlikely that he had these or any other reflections in mind as he penned his epic. In fact, I would be surprised if he gave any thought at all to how the themes of his story might instruct twenty-first-century readers. *The Lord of the Rings* is not, as some have suggested, a covert allegory of the gospel. Tolkien clearly denied that idea. We must not turn this wonderful adventure into something it was never intended to be. I agree with Clyde Kilby, who said that "no real lover of Tolkien's fiction would want it turned into sermons, no matter how cleverly preached."[3] Tolkien was telling a story, not proclaiming a message. His Christian worldview pushed itself up of its own accord.

It is not our goal to declare Tolkien's intentions, but rather to explore the inference of his imagination, an imagination that could not help but reflect Christian themes. It's in this context that Tolkien described his fantasy as a fundamentally religious work growing out of his own faith journey.[4] As with any artistic effort, what Tolkien believed was part of him, and that belief became part of what he created.

With that disclaimer, I invite you to reflect upon the Christian themes found throughout *The Lord of the Rings*. May the fantasy Tolkien created inspire us with the truths he believed.

Kurt Bruner

A DEEP YEARNING

The world was fair, the mountains tall
In Elder Days before the fall.
(Gimli's song—Book II, Chapter 4)

There is a deep yearning among the Fellowship of the Ring, an unspoken longing for something long lost. None have known it in their lifetimes. Few can recite the tales of its splendor. But all desire its discovery and hope to play a part in its restoration.

Throughout their adventure, characters from Bilbo to Treebeard recite verses of what they sense is an epic tale being told, a tale in which their lives somehow play a part. Each song seems to be merely a fragment of a majestic symphony being written and conducted by an all-knowing composer. But, as the chorus of Gimli reveals, something is wrong. Part of the harmony isn't right, like a dissonant chord invading the sweet melody of life, refusing resolution.

Middle-earth is in its third age as the adventures of the Fellowship begin. There is considerable history to this world, as revealed in the legends of Elder Days. Elves, dwarves, men, and hobbits alike know that theirs is a story that predates the present scene, preserved and passed in tales of ancient lore. Gimli's chorus tells of life "before the fall" when the beloved homeland of his dwarf ancestors was full of splendor and light, not dark and foreboding as they find it now. Gimli's heart pines for glories long past when his people knew better days, before the fall of their blessed domain.

A yearning heart is fitting. The wise know that before time was counted a rebellion occurred that brought evil into their world and introduced discord to the music of life. This rebellion was the driving force behind the song of the Dark Lord now heard in the march of orcs and the movements of the Black Riders. Awakened by the diminished sounds of beauty, honor, and goodness stubbornly pushing their way through the noisy clatter of evil, the inhabitants of Middle-earth hope for the day when all will again be set right.

⇥ ‡ ⇤

You and I, like Gimli and others of Tolkien's world, long for better days. We somehow know that our world is less than it was made to be. And we hope that it will one day be set right again. In short, we yearn for the goodness that was "before the fall."

Why do we find it so difficult to accept the world as it is? Are we merely discontent, or is something more profound at work in our hearts? C. S. Lewis believed that our desire for something better is a gift, a way of reminding us of what it is we lost and what it is we hope to regain. "Creatures are not born with desires unless satisfaction for those desires exists," Lewis explains. "A baby feels hunger: well, there is such a thing as food. A duckling wants to swim: well, there is such a thing as water. Men feel sexual desire: well, there is such a thing as sex. If I find in myself a desire which no experience in this world can satisfy, the most probable explanation is that I was made for another world."[5]

What is the real thing our yearnings suggest? Put simply,

it is goodness. We desire the kind of all-consuming goodness that we've never known but that once existed and will some-day be restored.

We live in a broken world. Death, pain, sickness, and suffering were not part of life's original melody. These dis-sonant chords were first introduced when our race took the bait of temptation and fell from its former glory. Once upon a time, mankind was offered a choice. We could sing the good song of the great composer or follow the opposing melody of his enemy. We chose the latter. And when we rejected the good that God is, we embraced the bad that he isn't.

Evil entered Tolkien's world before the dawn of time. That story, told in the opening pages of *The Silmarillion*, sets the stage for choices later made by those who would inhabit Middle-earth. It starts with Ilúvatar, maker of all that would be. His first creations were Ainur, angelic beings described as "the offspring of his thought." To each Ainur, Ilúvatar assigned themes of music that would be sung for his honor and pleasure.

> *Then Ilúvatar said to them: "Of the theme that I have declared to you, I will now that ye make in harmony together a Great Music . . . ye shall show forth your powers in adorning this theme, each with his own thoughts and devices, if he will. But I will sit and hearken, and be glad that through you great beauty has been wakened into song."*[6]

The beauty of their music is that for which all creation yearns. It is the original chorus which "the morning stars sang together and all the angels shouted for joy" as revealed to a suffering Job (Job 38:7). It is the true melody, the "good" that once was. It is the world as it was intended before the birth of evil. The story continues:

> But now Ilúvatar sat and hearkened, and for a great while it seemed good to him, for in the music there were no flaws. But as the theme progressed, it came into the heart of Melkor to interweave matters of his own imagining that were not in accord with the theme of Ilúvatar; for he sought therein to increase the power and glory of the part assigned to himself.[7]

Sadly, the sound of Melkor's evil theme increased as some "began to attune their music to his rather than to the thought which they had at first."

Seldom have more graceful words been penned to reflect a Christian understanding of Satan's revolt and its eventual impact upon God's creation. Tolkien's world, like ours, knows the dissonance of an opposing melody. It knows the insatiable appetite of a rebellion that seeks to destroy the good that should rightfully rule.

Tolkien saw our world as neither completely right nor completely wrong, but rather as a good that has been violated, a beauty marred. He realized that the only way we can understand that which occurs within time is to view it within the context of that which occurred before and beyond time.

Though our world is broken, there is good news. It will not always be so. The story of history, like that of Middle-earth, is progressing toward eventual redemption. Even that which seeks to undermine good will one day play a part in its restoration. As Ilúvatar foretold,

And thou, Melkor, shalt see that no theme may be played
that hath not its uttermost source in me, nor can any alter
the music in my despite. For he that attempteth this shall
prove but mine instrument in the devising of things more
wonderful, which he himself hath not imagined.[8]

And so Ilúvatar, after the pattern of the biblical Jehovah, produces a drama performed in the theater of time. Its story will become the visible expression of the Ainur's chorus, including the song of a simple hobbit and the discord of an evil rebel. And somehow, the former will resolve the latter.

∽ Reflection

OUR HEARTS YEARN FOR THE GOOD THAT GOD IS.

SMALL TALE

"I might find somewhere where I can finish my book. I have thought of a nice ending for it: *and he lived happily ever after to the end of his days.*"
(Bilbo to Gandalf—Book I, Chapter 1)

It was time. Bilbo Baggins of Bag End needed to leave the Shire. But it wasn't his style to slip away unnoticed under cover of darkness. After all, Bilbo was famous in these parts. A quiet departure just wouldn't do. A party was the thing, a celebration of Bilbo's life on the eve of his disappearance. And what better occasion than his 111th birthday? So, invitations sent and accepted, Bilbo hosted the biggest gala ever seen among the simple folk of Hobbiton.

There was much to celebrate. After all, it was quite unusual for a hobbit to live such a long and healthy life as Bilbo Baggins had. For some mysterious reason, he hadn't seemed to age a day since turning fifty. Though time had left its unkind mark on everyone else, an unexplained youthful vigor had remained with Bilbo ever since his return to Hobbiton. Perhaps the adventure of his younger days had brought with it more than mere wealth.

His quest had certainly given Bilbo Baggins a wonderful story to tell, a story he had been writing in his book. Whether many would ever read the book was of little concern to Bilbo. He simply felt the need to put it down so that future generations could know what happened to and through him. Sent off on a grand adventure at the bidding of Gandalf the wizard, Bilbo had acquired a magic ring. Though he didn't understand all of its powers, he knew that the ring was of great significance. When worn, it made him invisible, a very useful trick when fighting giant spiders or freeing jailed warriors. And it would be useful again as Bilbo planned to vanish from the Shire in style. Which he does, literally. At the end of his speech thanking those in attendance and bidding them good-bye, Bilbo Baggins disappears. He slips the magic ring on his finger and simply vanishes. He quite enjoys the trick and the animated talk it inspires.

With the fun over and Gandalf present to advise and guide, Bilbo knows that the final pages of his chapter are being turned. After he entrusts the Baggins fortune and magic ring to the keeping of his young nephew Frodo, it's time to leave.

He looks forward to the time he might now have to complete his book, a tale that Bilbo hopes will go on "happily ever after to the end of his days." But there's no way to know. Past adventures have taught him that the scenes of his life are serving a much bigger story than his could ever express. And while Bilbo may be the star of his tale, he is not its author.

⊰ ✦ ⊱

Once upon a time, we understood our lives to be part of a grand story being written by the divine author of history. But a dark yearning for autonomy and a nihilistic nudge from Nietzsche pushed us over the edge of sanity. God, the omniscient playwright, was declared dead. Now no one knows the plot to the epic drama in which we find ourselves, leaving us with competing small stories but no overarching narrative that frames and explains the seemingly random experiences of life.

Let's face it, we all wish we could write the scenes of our own stories. Like Bilbo Baggins, we want them to read "and he lived happily ever after to the end of his days." But deep down we know that we are not the authors of the events that shape our lives. Bilbo did not seek, and only reluctantly accepted, the invitation to adventure that launched his extra-ordinary tale of risk and reward. As Gandalf expressed to Bilbo in the closing conversation of *The Hobbit,* his quest had been orchestrated by another for a greater purpose.

> *Surely you don't disbelieve the prophecies, because you had a hand in bringing them about yourself? You don't really suppose, do you, that all your adventures and escapes were managed by mere luck, just for your sole benefit? You are a very fine person, Mr. Baggins, and I am very fond of you; but you are only quite a little fellow in a wide world after all!*[9]

Bilbo's adventure was part of a much bigger story that began long before his first breath and would continue well beyond his last. This realization elevated rather than minimized the importance of his part. But this could only happen if Mr. Baggins was honest and humble enough to embrace an important truth: that the big part he played in his small story was only a small part in the big story.

"My tongue is the pen of a skillful writer," writes the psalmist in Psalm 45:1, beautifully expressing a reality Bilbo learned and we would do well to recover. Bilbo knew he was not the author but the instrument. The pen does not become arrogant or proud over what is written on the page.

It is honored to have played any part at all in the creative act. It is when we struggle to take control and resist the author's intentions that we mar the story being told. Pride is not satisfied with anything less than the starring role. It grasps for more, seeking to write its own tale. But the humble heart has a very different view of life. It considers the warning "God resists the proud, but gives grace to the humble" (James 4:6, NKJV).

It heeds the admonition "Humble yourselves, therefore, under God's mighty hand. . . ."

And it reaps the benefits: ". . . that he may lift you up in due time" (1 Peter 5:6).

So, for hobbit and human alike, recognizing that our small stories serve a much larger purpose can turn ordinary details of the daily grind into scenes of an extraordinary adventure! And what better way for your "once upon a time" to discover its ultimate "happily ever after"?

⬎ Reflection
THE SCENES OF YOUR LIFE SERVE A STORY MUCH BIGGER THAN YOUR OWN.

THE CALL

"This ring! . . . How, how on earth
did it come to me?"
(Frodo to Gandalf—Book I, Chapter 2)

It had happened in just this same way to his uncle Bilbo,
Frodo reflected. Well, perhaps not *exactly* the same way;
but the similarities were striking. He had heard the story
many times from the old hobbit himself: Bilbo had been
standing outside the round green door to his hobbit hole one
fine morning, contentedly smoking a pipe and minding his
own business, when along came Gandalf. The result? Staid,
stolid, stay-at-home Bilbo had ended up doing unthinkable
things, things that no sensible, respectable Baggins would
ever have dreamed of doing. A Took, perhaps. But a
Baggins? Never.

And now this same Gandalf was back at Bag End again.
Sitting there before the fire in Frodo's study, puffing out
smoke rings, watching him out of thin-slitted, heavy-
lidded, bushy-browed eyes, waiting. Waiting for Frodo's
answer.

Frodo fingered the Ring where it lay in his pocket on the
end of its chain. It felt heavy, heavier than a small ring of
gold had any right to be. Far heavier than it had felt just
half an hour earlier. He stared into the fire's dying embers
and shivered, thinking over everything Gandalf had just
told him about this terrible ring. The One Ring. The Ring
of Power. Long believed lost, now earnestly and desperately
sought by its maker, the dreaded Dark Lord. The Ring that

threatened to overpower everyone and everything, to change Middle-earth forever. The Ring that had somehow landed in Frodo's pocket.

There is only one way, he heard Gandalf saying again. One way to save the Shire. One way to destroy the Ring before Sauron can seize it and use it for his own ends: Frodo must find Mount Orodruin in the dark land of Mordor and cast the cursed thing into the Cracks of Doom. And how was he—a simple hobbit of the Shire—supposed to do *that?*

Not that Frodo was a stay-at-home. He had often dreamed of traveling. He *wanted* to have adventures like old Uncle Bilbo. Like Bilbo, he had more of the Took than of the Baggins in him. That's why gossips in taverns had taken to calling both of them "cracked." Frodo was notoriously impractical. Images of pleasant, leisurely rambles and idyllic wanderings filled his mind at every idle moment. Many times he had pictured himself taking long, aimless journeys through endless woods, splashing across fabled rivers under the stars, conversing with elves.

But *this!* This was something else altogether. He was not made for perilous quests! He hadn't counted on taking his life in his hands and fleeing from danger to danger. Most of all, he hadn't planned on carrying the burden of the world in his waistcoat pocket. He wished now that he had never seen the horrid Ring! Why him? Why should he have been chosen to undertake such a task? When he had posed that question, he had received a most unsatisfactory reply from the inscrutable wizard: *You may be sure that it was not for any merit that others do not possess.*

"Well!" said Gandalf, looking up at last. "Have you decided what to do?"

⊨ ✝ ⊭

Every adventure has a beginning. Unfortunately, that beginning isn't always pleasant. It might be more in the nature of
a rude awakening. A prod, a sting, a shove. A bucket of cold
water in the face. The thing you least expected to happen.
The words you never wanted to hear. That's how it is, more
often than not, with those who find themselves on the
adventure of following the living Christ.

> As Jesus was walking beside the Sea of Galilee, he saw
> two brothers, Simon called Peter and his brother Andrew.
> They were casting a net into the lake, for they were fisher-
> men. "Come, follow me," Jesus said, "and I will make you
> fishers of men." At once they left their nets and followed
> him. (Matthew 4:18-20)

Fishers of *men?* They hadn't been expecting *that* when they
rolled out of bed that morning, pulled rough, homespun
tunics over their heads, and stumbled down to the lakeside
to work on those perpetually torn and shredded nets. Fishing for fish, now that was something they knew. But fishing
for men? What did it even mean? It was clearly out of their
line of work.

> As he walked along, he saw Levi son of Alphaeus sitting
> at the tax collector's booth. "Follow me," Jesus told him,
> and Levi got up and followed him. (Mark 2:14)

It was like a bolt out of the blue, unanticipated and totally
unpredictable. Imagine what must have been going through
Levi's mind as he turned his head at those thunderous words:
Is he talking to somebody else around here?

When Jesus reached the spot, he looked up and said to him, "Zacchaeus, come down immediately. I must stay at your house today." (Luke 19:5)

He had climbed a tree out of pure curiosity, just to watch the parade go by, and suddenly Zacchaeus found himself at the end of a pointing finger—an accusing finger, a forgiving finger, a defining, inescapable, Uncle Sam "I WANT YOU" finger. And down he came. (Lucky for him he didn't fall!)

Then, of course, there was Nathanael, the skeptic. He had been sitting under a fig tree, laughing in his beard—"Hah! A Messiah? From *Nazareth?* Give me a break!"—when suddenly he felt a little tap on the shoulder. "Here," said Jesus with a beckoning smile, "is a true Israelite, in whom there is nothing false." Nathanael probably did a double-take. "How do you know me?" he asked (John 1:46-48).

Rustic fishermen as ambassadors for the King of the Universe? A slimy, pocket-padding tax collector as an apostle for the gospel of righteousness? A cynic as a herald of the truth? Why them? One wonders whether these unlikely candidates for glory—as unlikely as a furry-footed halfling trudging determinedly and heroically down the road to Mordor—thought about the words of Moses, Gideon, and Jeremiah as they stood there confronting the Christ Who Lets No One off the Hook: "O LORD, please send someone else to do it!" (Exodus 4:13); "But LORD . . . how can I save Israel? My clan is the weakest in Manasseh, and I am the least in my family!" (Judges 6:15); "Ah, Sovereign LORD . . . I do not know how to speak; I am only a child" (Jeremiah 1:6).

In every case there was reluctance, resistance, protest. In every case the chosen one made a manful attempt to beg off. But in every case the ultimate response was the same: "They left their nets and followed him." "Levi got up and followed him." "He came down at once and welcomed him gladly." "Nathanael declared, 'Rabbi, you are the Son of God; you are the King of Israel.' "

It says volumes about the irresistible power, the inescapable attraction, the captivating, compelling personality of the one who issued the call to adventure: "Come, follow me!"

And so it was with Frodo. As he felt the weight of the Ring on the palm of his small hand, as he trembled inside, staring into the glowing embers and picturing the fabled fires of Orodruin, it dawned on him that, for all the danger, for all the terror, for all the unthinkable labor and pain it might involve, there simply was *no other choice*. And though he felt "very small, and very uprooted, and . . . desperate," he knew he had to go.

What about you? Have you decided what to do?

∽ *Reflection*

THE CALL TO FOLLOW CHRIST IS A CALL TO ADVENTURE—INCONVENIENT, IMPERIOUS, AND IRRESISTIBLE.

EVIL INTENTIONS

"But we must do something, soon.
The Enemy is moving."
(Gandalf to Frodo—Book I, Chapter 2)

Things had rarely been so good in the Shire. Many years had passed since the disappearance of Mr. Bilbo Baggins, an event that had achieved legendary stature among those living in the Shire village of Hobbiton. But life had returned to normal, and few gave much thought to the meaning of such strange happenings.

Bilbo's nephew Frodo had inherited the magic ring from his departing uncle. Warned years earlier by the wise Gandalf against its use, he knew of its mystical powers and mysterious dangers. But the Ring's mere presence created a forbidding sense of unwelcome destiny for Frodo Baggins. More recently, that sense included news that suggested trouble on the horizon. There were many signs: elves walking through the Shire and leaving their homeland for good, rumors of strange events beyond the peaceful border of the Shire, and refugee dwarves fleeing west and whispering of an enemy arising from the land of Mordor. Change was definitely in the wind, and not for the better.

But it was not until the arrival of Gandalf, who returned after years abroad, that Frodo learned the details. Trouble was indeed coming, and it was seeking Frodo. More precisely, it was seeking that which he held. As Gandalf explained, the Ring Bilbo had acquired and passed to Frodo was the one of which ancient songs and folklore told. It was the Ring of

Doom, so potent that, if possessed, it would enable the dark powers of evil to rule the whole of Middle-earth. These dark powers had previously had little knowledge of or concern for hobbits. But they had followed the Ring's trail and knew it to be in the Shire in the keeping of Baggins. As Gandalf explained, the enemy was on the move, and the Ring-bearer, Frodo, was the target.

⊰ ✝ ⊱

The true forces of evil in our world are rarely haphazard or indiscriminate. The occasional mad gunman notwith-standing, the history of mankind shows that the most destructive wickedness is devious and determined. Violent insanity is far less trouble than diabolical brilliance. While a violent lunatic may murder dozens, a calculating Adolf Hitler convinced ordinary people to systematically extermi-nate millions.

Evil has intention. It targeted Frodo Baggins as a means to an end. He possessed an object that the evil ruler Sauron wanted, an object that could give Sauron the power to enslave all others. His burning desire for revenge and con-suming lust for domination drove Sauron to set very specific goals in pursuit of his ultimate objective. He did not order the destruction of all that lived in the Shire. He ordered the pursuit of Baggins, the bearer of the Ring through which he would enslave the Shire.

The Christian worldview is far from naïve or simplistic with regard to evil. It understands the existence and nature of an enemy set upon our enslavement and ultimate destruction. Just as there is a person called Sauron who is part of a con-spiracy invading the happy world of hobbits, there is a rebel called Lucifer whose calculating schemes invade the lives of men. We have been told of his history and intentions.

We know he was once a trusted servant in the heavenly realm.

> You were in Eden, the garden of God; every precious stone adorned you. . . . Your settings and mountings were made of gold; on the day you were created they were prepared. You were anointed as a guardian cherub, for so I ordained you. You were on the holy mount of God; you walked among the fiery stones. You were blameless in your ways from the day you were created till wickedness was found in you. (Ezekiel 28:13-15)

We know that he led a rebellion in hopes of assuming the throne of his creator.

> You said in your heart, "I will ascend to heaven; I will raise my throne above the stars of God; I will sit enthroned on the mount of assembly, on the utmost heights of the sacred mountain. I will ascend above the tops of the clouds; I will make myself like the Most High." (Isaiah 14:13-14)

We know that he was defeated and exiled, cast out of heaven due to insane pride.

> I banished you from the mountain of God. I expelled you, O mighty guardian, from your place among the stones of fire. (Ezekiel 28:16, NLT)

> I saw Satan fall like lightning from heaven. (Luke 10:18)

We know that he seeks revenge by enslaving and destroying God's beloved children—and that, like Frodo, we cannot afford the luxury of complacency.

> *Be self-controlled and alert. Your enemy the devil prowls around like a roaring lion looking for someone to devour. (1 Peter 5:8)*

> *Put on all of God's armor so that you will be able to stand firm against all strategies and tricks of the Devil. For we are not fighting against people made of flesh and blood, but against the evil rulers and authorities of the unseen world, against those mighty powers of darkness who rule this world, and against wicked spirits in the heavenly realms. (Ephesians 6:11-12, NLT)*

Lucifer, the personal force behind the most destructive evil in our world, is very intentional about his plan for revenge and domination. We must therefore be on our guards and prepare ourselves to overcome obstacles that we will certainly face while on the great adventure of living by faith.

⮌ *Reflection*
EVIL IS NEITHER PASSIVE NOR COMPLACENT.
IT IS PERSONAL, AND IT IS ACTIVELY DETERMINED
TO DOMINATE OUR LIVES.

WISE COUNSEL

"Do be careful of that Ring, Frodo."
(Gandalf to Frodo—Book I, Chapter 1)

Frodo Baggins had become keeper of the Ring, a burden inherited from his long departed uncle. With little understanding of its history or power, Frodo found the Ring to be a thing of great mystery, as likely to be a source of trouble as good. But one thing was certain: it needed to be handled with great care. After all, Gandalf himself had cautioned against its use.

Frodo was a relatively young hobbit when he first began to heed the counsel of Gandalf. For some reason, the wise wizard demonstrated great respect for and fear of the Ring, discerning more of its significance than most. And so, against the natural inclination of youth, Frodo suppressed his desire to explore its powers. Instead, he kept it safely hidden and unworn until another encounter with Gandalf many years later when, like his uncle Bilbo, Frodo would be summoned to his own great adventure.

The wisdom of Gandalf would be a critical source of guidance for Frodo throughout his life. From an unsettling first conversation shortly after Bilbo's disappearance to life-and-death choices made while confronting the forces of darkness, Frodo gleaned great insight whenever he listened to his friend, mentor, and counselor—insight he would have missed had he allowed the arrogance of youth or the self-satisfaction of pride to get in the way of that vital skill of the wise: the willingness to learn from those wiser still.

There would be others besides Gandalf, such as Aragorn. Also known as Strider, Aragorn became a faithful guide through treacherous journeys. Frodo's most loyal companions did not trust this haggard-looking ranger at first. But Frodo looked deeper and gained much. And then there was the great Elrond, counselor to the wise, who gave refuge and guidance to all on the side of good. There was also Galadriel, the Lady of Lórien, whose long gaze and admonition tested the deepest intentions of Frodo's heart. The collective wisdom of these and others gave Frodo the direction needed to carry out a quest that would ultimately place this simple hobbit among the greatest heroes in the history of Middle-earth.

⊰ ✝ ⊱

Anyone willing to become ignorant can become wise. It is only when we humble ourselves by acknowledging that we don't know everything that we are able to learn from others. And learning from others is the great talent of the truly wise.

Socrates was called the father of philosophy, a man for whom the pursuit of wisdom became all-consuming. According to the writings of his student and biographer, Plato, Socrates became wise through recognition of his own ignorance. In fact, his greatest criticism was of men who considered themselves too wise to learn from others. "Although I do not suppose that either of us knows anything really beautiful and good," said Socrates, "I am better off than he is, —for he knows nothing, and thinks that he knows; I neither know nor think that I know."[10] His approach to learning was simple: Ask questions of others. Sometimes he discovered that those we might consider wise are really fools. But the process of listening taught him much nonetheless.

Frodo didn't pretend to possess the wisdom necessary to accomplish the quest for which he had been chosen. When others spoke, he listened. He did not, as is often our error, seek to impress anyone with his own superior knowledge. Frodo was humble enough to learn from those wiser still, recognizing that truth is something we discover, not something we define.

Contrast the example of Frodo Baggins with what has become the mantra of our generation. From New Age gurus and pop psychologists to hit songs and blockbuster movies, the messages we receive follow the same basic melody:

> *Listen to your feelings.*
> *Look within for answers.*
> *Follow your heart.*
> *Get in touch with your own higher consciousness.*

This collective chorus says that I am my own source of truth and wisdom. The problem is not that I am listening too little, but that I am listening too much. When I heed teachings and wisdom from the past—such as what I learn from the church—I risk suppressing my own personal, customized truth.

Some messages are less subtle, like the message of Neale Donald Walsch, who in his best-selling book *Conversations with God* boldly declares, "The soul—your soul—knows all there is to know all the time. There's nothing hidden to it, nothing unknown."[11] Funny, we didn't know *that!*

The collective message of our generation runs counter to the wisdom of hobbits and the admonition of Scripture.

Let the wise listen and add to their learning, and let the discerning get guidance—for understanding proverbs and parables, the sayings and riddles of the wise.
(Proverbs 1:5-6)

Middle-earth had its own proverbs, parables, sayings, and riddles of the wise. They took the form of poems and songs. Frodo's counselors often recited their verses of ancient lore as they sought guidance for the present adventure. None looked within for hidden knowledge; instead, they looked back to what had already been revealed. As a result, they learned much, including the dark purpose of the One Ring. Most important, they knew the peril of joining the song of the one who had rebelled against the creator. After all, in their world as in ours, "The fear of the LORD is the beginning of wisdom; all who follow his precepts have good understanding" (Psalm 111:10).

⮑ Reflection

WE BECOME WISE WHEN WE HUMBLE OURSELVES TO HEED THE COUNSEL OF THOSE WHO HAVE GONE BEFORE.

DECEPTIVE APPEARANCES

All that is gold does not glitter,
Not all those who wander are lost.
(Book I, Chapter 10)

THE PRANCING PONY BY BARLIMAN BUTTERBUR—so read the sign over the door in large white letters. The Pony was the only inn in Bree. And it wasn't the sort of inn where hobbits from the Shire could feel absolutely comfortable about spending the night. Sam didn't like the look of it at all. It was three stories high and had bedrooms on every floor. No hobbit likes to sleep above the ground.

Old Barliman, the innkeeper, was reassuring. Careful and cautious, perhaps. Definitely a bit scattered and overly harried. But he was friendly enough and hospitable to a fault. He made the four weary travelers feel right at home.

If only the same could have been said of the other guests they found gathered in the Common Room that night! *They* were a wild and rough-cut-looking bunch. Outlandish and strange, "strange as news from Bree," as the saying was. There were the local Bree-men, Big People with whom the Shire hobbits rarely had dealings, and the hobbits of Bree, halflings indeed, yet different enough from their kin to the west to raise respectable eyebrows back in Hobbiton and Bywater. A number of dwarves sat at Barliman's table, too, having come a long journey west along the Great Road from over the Misty Mountains. And there were mysterious travelers from the South, humans who had come up the Greenway only the previous afternoon, a couple of them rather ill-favored, sallow-faced, and suspicious-looking. It was enough to make a decent hobbit fidget and squirm.

But strangest and most forbidding of all was the tall, dark man who sat smoking a long pipe back in a shadowy corner. He was wrapped in a dark green cloak. A voluminous hood hid his face in shadows. High, well-worn, mud-caked boots covered the lower shanks of his long legs. A Ranger, Barliman had called him, a solitary wanderer who came and went at will and kept his business a mystery. It was clear that everybody felt a little shy of him. Worst of all, Frodo had the feeling that the man was watching him.

It wasn't long before that feeling was confirmed. As Frodo passed him, the dark man threw back his hood, looked him straight in the eye, and spoke in a low but alarmingly intense voice. "If I were you," he said, "I should stop your young friends from talking too much. . . . There are queer folk about."

Frodo didn't say what he was thinking: that this Strider—for such was his name—was the queerest of them all.

Who would have guessed that this odd bird would end up as advisor, leader, guide, and protector to the four vulnerable travelers from the Shire? Who in his wildest dreams would have supposed that this tramping traveler was a king incognito? And yet that's exactly the way it turned out. It all began when forgetful old Barliman finally recalled something he had been trying to remember ever since the hobbits showed up on his doorstep. It was a letter from Gandalf.

"You may meet a friend of mine on the Road," the letter read, "a Man, lean, dark, tall, by some called Strider. He knows our business and will help you." In a postscript was appended a snatch of verse:

All that is gold does not glitter,
Not all those who wander are lost . . .

That was all the convincing Frodo needed; though even before the letter came to light, a feeling had been growing upon him that this Strider, Aragorn son of Arathorn, was, after all, a friend.

> *"You have frightened me several times tonight," Frodo explained, "but never in the way that servants of the Enemy would, or so I imagine. I think one of his spies would—well, seem fairer and feel fouler, if you understand."*

Apparently Strider did. He laughed in reply.

≺ ✝ ≻

"All that glitters is not gold," runs the old saying. The verse that Gandalf quotes turns that proverb on its head: "All that is gold does not glitter."

Beauty is only skin deep. Yes, but so is ugliness. Appearances can be deceiving. And for those who set out on the adventure of faith, it's vital to understand that the deception can work both ways. To know what you're really looking at, you have to be able to see with the eyes of the heart.

We know that the devil can appear as an angel of light (2 Corinthians 11:14). Anyone who has been around the block a few times is probably wise enough to mistrust an attractive veneer. The smooth-talking salesman in the flawless three-piece suit; the slick-haired televangelist; the friendly solicitor with the perfect smile—there's a reason they make us uncomfortable. They seem fair but *feel* foul. Somehow we can't shake a nagging suspicion that the bright, unblemished exterior is too good to be true, that it's a smoke screen, an overlay, an affectation assumed to conceal ulterior motives. And how many sad love songs and tragic romances does it take to teach us that a pretty face can conceal a cold, deceitful heart?

There's a similar theme embedded in many of the old folk and fairy tales. Until Snow White came of age, her wicked stepmother was unrivaled as "the fairest in the land." The White Witch who holds sway over C. S. Lewis's Narnia is pale and cold but perilously beautiful. So is Hans Christian Andersen's Snow Queen, a lovely lady in white furs who sweeps young Kay away to her soul-deadening, heart-chilling fastness in the North. The message is clear: Outward loveliness can be a screen for deep-seated evil. To use Jesus' image, a whitewashed tomb may conceal a pile of rank and rotting bones.

But the deception of appearance can be a double-cutting blade. What about the other edge? Can something *look* foul and yet be fair? Is it possible that God sends his most precious gifts to us in packages we are little tempted to open? Can truth and beauty be concealed behind an unattractive— even repulsive—veneer?

That's the way it happened in Strider's case. And in this sense, Tolkien's king incognito reflects a fundamental biblical principle. He is, in an important way, modeled on a series of biblical archetypes, a series that culminates in the Archetype of all archetypes: Jesus Christ himself.

Consider David.

God instructed the prophet Samuel to go down to Bethlehem and anoint one of Jesse's sons to be the next king. Seven

of them stood before him in order, all of impressive height
and build:

> When they arrived, Samuel saw Eliab and thought,
> "Surely the LORD's anointed stands here before the LORD."
> But the LORD said to Samuel, "Do not consider his appear-
> ance or his height, for I have rejected him. The LORD does
> not look at the things man looks at. Man looks at the out-
> ward appearance, but the LORD looks at the heart."
> (1 Samuel 16:6-7)

Samuel is stymied. "Are these all the sons you have?" he asks.

> "There is still the youngest," Jesse answered, "but he is
> tending the sheep." Samuel said, "Send for him." (v. 11)

And David the shepherd boy—the last, littlest, and least
likely to succeed of eight boys—is selected to become shepherd of God's people.

Who would have thought it? Who could have guessed?
An obscure tender of livestock, king of Israel? A swaddled
baby in a cave; a village carpenter with dirty fingernails; a
convicted criminal: King of the Universe? Not many did
catch it. But a few—themselves not the likeliest bunch who
ever lived—somehow had the eyes of faith to see behind
the disguise. The King walked among us, sat at our table,
broke bread in our presence; but, in the words of the old
spiritual, we didn't know who he was.

> He grew up before him like a tender shoot, and like a root
> out of dry ground. He had no beauty or majesty to attract
> us to him, nothing in his appearance that we should desire

him. He was despised and rejected by men, a man of sorrows, and familiar with suffering. Like one from whom men hide their faces he was despised, and we esteemed him not. (Isaiah 53:2-3)

✎ Reflection

LOOK CLOSELY! GOOD AND EVIL SELDOM COME CLEARLY LABELED.

SHUTTING OUT THE NIGHT

"Come, dear folk . . . Laugh and be merry. . . .
Let us shut out the night. Fear nothing!"
(Goldberry to the hobbits—Book I, Chapter 7)

The Old Forest had lived up to its reputation. Since childhood, Frodo, Sam, Pippin, and Merry had heard only the most appalling, bone-chilling stories about the place. Nothing could have persuaded Sam and Pippin to set out under its dark eaves had they not known that their dear Mr. Frodo was being pursued by an even graver, more sinister danger. If they were to escape at all, they would have to resort to secrecy and surprise. And so Merry, practical and sensible Merry, had suggested it: the road through the Old Forest. The path nobody ever took and nobody would ever expect them to take. The path they would have refused after all . . . if only they had known.

They *hadn't* known for sure. They had only had their fears. But as things turned out, those fears were more than justified. The Old Forest wasn't just dark and forbidding, it was hostile! It was a thinking, scheming, living organism (or so it seemed), bent on their destruction. That's how it happened that, try as they might, they simply could not strike a course due north in the direction of the great East Road. Instead, the farther they went, the more they found themselves inexorably deflected and driven southeast, toward the Withywindle valley, source and center of everything that made the Old Forest such a terrifying place.

It wasn't long before Sam and Frodo found themselves confronting the unthinkable. Their two companions had been swallowed alive! By a tree! Lulled to sleep and—*snap!*—caught within the gaping cracks of the gnarled, massive trunk of the malicious Old Willow and squeezed nearly in two. Frodo and Sam had no idea how to rescue their friends.

And then hope met them unexpectedly. Hope came skipping and dancing down the path as if out of nowhere. Hope in a battered, feather-topped hat, a blue coat, and a pair of tall yellow boots. It was old Tom Bombadil, master of water, wood, and hill! Bombadil, that strange old leaping, capering sprite!

With a song he freed the helpless prisoners and led them, still trembling from their brush with disaster, to the comfort and refuge of his own house. It was a place filled with light, music, mirth, and—most important to a hobbit's way of thinking—food and drink. Food for the body and refreshment for the soul.

"Come, dear folk," said Tom's wife, Goldberry, the River-daughter, as she greeted the wide-eyed hobbits at the door. To them she appeared as great a marvel as Tom himself: yellow-haired, green-gowned, young and fair but ancient and wise. Just to stand in her presence was to feel the strength of an unshakable joy, the joy of knowing and celebrating one's place in the grand scheme of the world. "Fear nothing!" she laughed, as she showed them the way inside. "For tonight you are under the roof of Tom Bombadil."

And so they followed her, dropping their fears at the threshold with their baggage. There, under the roof of Tom Bombadil, the weary and shaken travelers ate and sang and laughed and talked until their troubles faded into distant memory. After that they slept a deep, renewing sleep while the rain drummed on the roof above their heads. And as long as they were under that roof, they almost forgot that there was anything to fear.

⊰ ‡ ⊱

Tolkien's Middle-earth, to borrow Yeats's famous phrase, is a place of "terrible beauty," a realm of breathtaking splendor, suffused with a sense of ever-present peril. It's a land where the sunset glow edging the delicate green leaves with red-gold is all the more beautiful, all the more precious, because one knows that the darkness is never far away. It's a glorious world, inhabited by many fearsome things.

Middle-earth, in other words, is a hauntingly luminous mirror image of *our* world. For we know that the world in which we live is a perilous place, a place where good and bad, light and dark, innocence and horror, glory and depravity march side by side and sleep back-to-back. We forget this at times, of course. In the course of our dull daily routines we often grow numbly accustomed to it all. But there are those moments when we wake suddenly in the middle of the night and remember that we are, after all, surrounded by terrors.

This is what it means to live in the midst of a fallen creation. God made the world and called it good (Genesis 1:31). We resonate with that goodness every time we gaze in awe at snowcapped mountain peaks, feel the tingle of sea spray in our nostrils, or tremble at the touch of a human hand. But the goodness is no longer unadulterated; it was marred when sin and disobedience entered the world. And

now creation literally aches to be released from the conse-
quences of its blemish and disease:

> *The creation was subjected to frustration, not by its own
> choice, but by the will of the one who subjected it, in hope
> that the creation itself will be liberated from its bondage
> to decay. (Romans 8:20-21)*

> *Sin entered the world through one man, and death through
> sin, and in this way death came to all men, because all
> sinned. (Romans 5:12)*

It's just as we suspected. All is *not* well. Creation, once so
bright and pure, is out of kilter. And dark things walk
abroad. No wonder we tremble as we walk through the
world, just as Sam, Frodo, Merry, and Pippin trembled as
they traversed the shadows of the Old Forest. Those who
don't tremble don't know. They're asleep or drugged or
hiding with their heads in the sand.

Into the midst of this bleak scenario come two little
words, as stunning in their effect as two bolts of lighting:
"Fear not." It's one of the most oft-repeated commandments
in all of Scripture:

> *Have I not commanded you? Be strong and courageous.
> Do not be terrified; do not be discouraged. (Joshua 1:9)*

> *Immediately Jesus spoke to them, saying, "Take courage,
> it is I; do not be afraid." (Matthew 14:27, NASB)*

> *The angel said to them, "Do not be afraid; for behold,
> I bring you good news of great joy." (Luke 2:10, NASB)*

> *He placed his right hand on me and said: "Do not be
> afraid. I am the First and the Last." (Revelation 1:17)*

"Don't be afraid." It's a command that begs a nagging question: Isn't it a bit naïve and Pollyannaish to cast all fear aside? Should we really, like the hobbits in old Bombadil's house, laugh and sing the night away while just beyond the door the Wargs prowl and the scythe-edged winds howl and the Barrow-wights stalk the bleak, deserted downs? Is it really possible to "shut out the night"? Who but a fool or a silly child can take those two little words "fear not" seriously?

None but a child indeed. It's no accident that the *real* heroes of Tolkien's dangerous, epic-proportioned world are hobbits, "halflings" to the men of Rohan and Gondor, creatures who walk among the larger-than-life-sized elves and warriors and wizards of Middle-earth like toddlers through a crowd of adults. Hobbits, for all their subtleties, are folk of a trusting and dependent nature, of plain and simple tastes. Hobbits are easily enchanted and carried away. Under the spell of Tom's boisterous cheerfulness and Goldberry's fairness and grace, they quickly put anxiety aside.

And so it was that, under the roof of Tom Bombadil, in the living, leaping presence of the goodness of all things made, under the influence of love and grace poured out in the shape of bread and meat and ale and downy soft beds, Frodo, Sam, Pippin, and Merry forgot their fears and found new strength for their journey. In that house they did indeed succeed in "shutting out the night." For no night, no matter how dark, could ever eclipse the ancient, primeval light, the solid, unshakable joy that received them there.

> Do not be afraid; for behold, I bring you good news of great joy. (Luke 2:10, NASB)

> Nehemiah said, "Go and enjoy choice food and sweet drinks, and send some to those who have nothing

prepared. . . . Do not grieve, for the joy of the LORD is
your strength." (Nehemiah 8:10)

There is no fear in love. But perfect love drives out fear.
(1 John 4:18)

Reflection

FEAR IS CONQUERED AND STRENGTH RENEWED
AS WE CELEBRATE THE GOODNESS OF GOD'S
CREATION AND LUXURIATE IN HIS LOVE.

HIDDEN COURAGE

There is a seed of courage hidden . . .
waiting for some final and desperate danger
to make it grow.
(Book I, Chapter 8)

Refreshed and encouraged after time in the house of
Tom Bombadil, Frodo and his friends resumed their journey. Departing farewells brought a strange mix of happy
sadness: happy for the rescue and friendship found, sad to
leave such a joyous setting. Too brief, their visit had been
a gift to weary spirits, a warm security not felt since leaving
the Shire. But it was time to go.

As the friends moved from sunlight to shadows, an
increasing fog decreased their visibility. Each step of their
journey took them away from the rich colors of western
safety into the pale gray of eastern danger. Sam, Pippin, and
Merry followed Frodo through the mist, donning cloaks and
hoods to protect them from the chilled, moist air. Suddenly,
Frodo turned and saw that he was alone. Hoping they had
simply failed to keep up, but fearing something worse, he
called out their names. All he could hear in reply was a faint
voice in the distance, perhaps a cry for help. Frantic, he
climbed the summit of a hill in the direction of the voice.
The ascension unveiled a dark sky and the faint light of
stars through the dissipating mist. Atop the hill loomed the
dark shape of a great barrow-wight waiting for Frodo's
approach. Its cold eyes peered at the hobbit just before it
seized him in its harsh grasp.

When Frodo woke from unconsciousness, he found himself captured by one of the Barrow-wights. Their repute, revealed in whispered tales, was of evil spirits that entrapped people to use in sacrifice. Frodo felt himself overtaken with great fear. He noticed Merry, Pippin, and Sam lying unconscious, or perhaps dead, at his side. A great sword was stretched across their throats. Frodo thought his quest had come to a dreadful end. Hope seemed gone. But rather than despair, Frodo found a seed of courage rising within. He thought of his uncle Bilbo and their many conversations about adventure. Bravery grows when facing desperate danger, enabling even simple hobbits to emerge victorious from great hazards.

His first thought was to use the Ring. Perhaps he could vanish and slip away unnoticed, saving himself at least. After all, he was not entirely certain that his companions were alive. Even Gandalf would likely agree such an act was necessary. But Frodo could not abandon his friends so easily. And so, drawing upon a bravery he didn't know he had, Frodo remained to face whatever would come in order to free his company.

This would not be the last or greatest terror to test Frodo's heart. Often, over the course of his adventure, he would be confronted with the choice between self-preservation and self-sacrifice. And as in this instance, pushing through great fear, Frodo repeatedly chose risk over retreat in order to accomplish the heroic quest to which he had been called.

⊰ ✝ ⊱

Of all the peoples of Middle-earth, none enjoyed life's comforts more than the hobbits. They slept longer, ate more frequently, and partied more merrily than others—a race better suited to friendly chats than deadly perils. A big part of the reason Frodo's courage is so inspiring is its contrast to his culture. His upbringing nurtured the pursuit of happy ease, not glorious adventure. That was the stuff of warrior dwarves like Gimli and rugged Rangers like Strider, not simple hobbits like Frodo. But the quest of the Ring showed everyone that even the smallest, least likely person was made for more than comfort and safety. We were made to be heroic.

Have you ever wondered why our favorite stories tend to include an ordinary person overcoming great odds to accomplish something extraordinary? It's because the capacity and desire to be heroic resides deep within each of us. And while we may avoid risk and deaden passion through our culture of affluence, the seed of courage remains within. We're reminded of its presence when we watch a nice guy named Rocky Balboa beat the arrogant champ Apollo Creed. Our hearts thrill when a young, inexperienced Luke Skywalker destroys the plans of the mighty Darth Vader. From a simpleton named Forrest Gump to a braveheart named William Wallace, we love to see the unlikely underdog beat the odds, hoping our own heroic nature would emerge if facing a similar challenge.

But no matter how hidden it may be, each of us has been given the capacity to overcome fear and apathy in order to play a heroic part in the scenes of life. For a timid farmer named Gideon, it was to lead hundreds in a battle against thousands. For newly elected member of Parliament William Wilberforce, it was to spend twenty years fighting the evil yet highly profitable British slave trade. For brave Allied soldiers, it was to free occupied Europe by storming the beaches of Normandy. For a black woman named Rosa Parks, it was to oppose racism by sitting in the front of a segregated bus. For young teacher Anne Sullivan, it was to patiently love Helen Keller out of dark silence.

The most renowned true story reflecting this reality is that of a boy named David. A young shepherd with no military experience, David volunteered to confront Goliath, the mighty giant of Gath. All of Saul's men, including David's older brothers, had refused the call to fight Goliath. But David knew that his life was about more than his own personal safety, and that sometimes the smallest and least likely are called to do more than any expect they can do. And so he raised his hand when others wouldn't, gathered five smooth stones, and confronted the enemy of good. And the rest, as they say, is history.

Living by faith includes the call to something greater than cowardly self-preservation.

> *For God did not give us a spirit of timidity, but a spirit of power, of love and of self-discipline.* (2 Timothy 1:7)

It is the invitation to water the seed of courage found deep within your heart. It inspires the passionless dulled by comfort and ease to resist the urge to place personal safety and preservation above the call to adventure, and instead, to become a hero.

⬲ Reflection
WE WERE MADE TO BE HEROIC.

THE LAST HOMELY HOUSE

"We have reached Rivendell, but the Ring
is not yet at rest."
(Gandalf to Frodo—Book II, Chapter 1)

Frodo awoke not knowing where he was. The bed was soft,
the rafters above his head were richly carved—Elvin work,
no doubt. There was sunlight in the room and the sound of
running water outside. He stirred, sat up, and caught his
breath. The wound in his shoulder was healing; he could
move his arm again! And who was this at his bedside? Was it
possible? It was! None other than old Gandalf himself! There
he sat, watching Frodo judiciously and puffing out smoke
rings that lazily wreathed his head before finding their way
to the paneled ceiling.

What place was this, and how had he come there? Of
this he had no recollection. All he could recall was the feeling of faintness and fear—piercing, cold, suffocating fear.
Then it came back to him: the desperate flight across the
Ford of Bruinen, with the bells of Glorfindel's horse jin-
gling furiously under him and the Nine Riders, cold, gray,
burning-eyed wraiths, hard on his trail. There had been a
flood, he remembered. He could still picture the river rising in crested waves that looked like wild, angry horses
with long, flowing manes. And flames of white fire. And
the din of crashing foam, and a cacophony of terrible cries.
And then . . . nothing.

And now? Well, it was apparent—how, he had no idea—
that the danger was past, at least for the time being, and that

he had indeed reached Rivendell at last. The long hoped for, but often despaired of, goal of their journey's first leg. Rivendell. The House of Elrond Halfelven. The Last Homely House east of the Sundering Seas.

And what a house it was! As Sam said of it, "There's something of everything here!" It was a place of many meetings, many glad reunions, many happy surprises. A place to sleep and eat and grow strong, to steep oneself in fellowship with the good, the noble, and the wise. A house of healing, refreshment, renewal, and desperately needed rest. Rivendell was a haven of light in a world that was growing darker by the day. Best of all, it was a citadel of Elven-lore, a repository of the old songs and stories, almost the last of its kind in Middle-earth.

Never afterwards would Sam or Frodo forget the night they sat in Elrond's Hall of Fire amongst elves and elf-friends and listened to old Bilbo chant a song of his own composition about Eärendil, the father of Elrond. "Eärendil was a mariner," the song began; an intercessor on behalf of Elves and Men, who sailed away into the West with the Silmaril on his brow to plead for help against the gathering Darkness. He never returned; for

> *on him mighty doom was laid,*
> *till Moon should fade, an orbèd star*
> *to pass, and tarry never more*
> *on Hither Shores where mortals are.*

Frodo might well have thought about Eärendil the next day when he stood in the Council of Elrond and took an equally "mighty doom" upon himself: the doom of bearing the One Ring into the heart of Mordor and casting it into the fires of

Orodruin. He may well have felt bitter and sorrowful at having to forsake Rivendell, house of ease and joy, for the hard, hard road that lay ahead. How pleasant it would have been to stay there forever, talking and reminiscing with Bilbo and helping him write his book! But he knew he could not stay. Later, a similar choice would confront the company in the Golden Wood, Lothlórien. And Sam would sum the situation up with characteristic simplicity:

> I've never heard of a better land than this. It's like being at home and on a holiday at the same time, if you understand me. I don't want to leave. All the same, I'm beginning to feel that if we've got to go on, then we'd best get it over.

Rivendell, Gandalf had said, was like a fortress in the midst of a darkening world; but if the Ring-bearer did not set out, the darkness would soon engulf Rivendell itself. Frodo knew that very well. He knew that Rivendell was not the journey's end. It was just an inn along the way—not the goal of the Quest, but a way station without which the Quest would have been unachievable. As Gandalf had said on that day when Frodo first awoke to find the wizard sitting by his side, "We have reached Rivendell, but the Ring is not yet at rest."

❧ ✟ ❧

Racers make pit stops. Boxers take a breather at the end of every round. Travelers look eagerly for inns and resting places along the highway. An oasis along the route of a desert journey can make the difference between life and death. But the traveler who has a specific goal in mind must be ready to leave the comfort of the way station when the right time comes. To mistake the inn for the journey's end is to fail altogether. It's to play into the enemy's hand.

There are many stories about questing wayfarers who got stuck somewhere along the road to their destination. Odysseus and his men were seduced into forgetfulness and lethargy by the comforts of the Land of the Lotus Eaters. Odysseus was the only man of that entire crew who ever made it back to Ithaca. The founding of Rome was long delayed while Aeneas enjoyed the alluring hospitality of Queen Dido. Of all the Knights of the Round Table who took the quest of the Holy Grail, only Galahad achieved the goal; most of the others allowed themselves to be deflected from their purpose, some by the perilously delightful temptation of rest and temporal enjoyments along the way. And then there were the children of Israel, who spent forty years making a journey that should have taken less than a month. Except for Joshua and Caleb, not a single man of that generation ever reached the Promised Land.

A temptation lay hidden behind the peace, comfort, and security of Rivendell. Without these benefits, Frodo would never have grown well and strong enough to make the trek to Mordor. But it required clarity of vision, sober-mindedness, and strength of will for him to leave them behind when duty called.

The House of Elrond was not the final destination, not even for the elves who dwelt there. To everyone who stopped there, the place supplied a taste of the immortal life beyond the sundering seas. But it was not Elven-home. It was like the taste of heavenly existence that Peter, James, and John got when they accompanied Jesus to the top of the Mount of Transfiguration: not an end in itself, but a moment of inspiration, intended to infuse them with strength for service in the valley below.

> About eight days after Jesus said this, he took Peter, John and James with him and went up onto a mountain to pray. As he was praying, the appearance of his face changed, and his clothes became as bright as a flash of lightning. Two men, Moses and Elijah, appeared in glorious splendor, talking with Jesus. They spoke about his departure, which he was about to bring to fulfillment at Jerusalem. Peter and his companions were very sleepy, but when they became fully awake, they saw his glory and the two men standing with him. As the men were leaving Jesus, Peter said to him, "Master, it is good for us to be here. Let us put up three shelters—one for you, one for Moses and one for Elijah." (He did not know what he was saying.) (Luke 9:28-33)

Peter may not have known exactly what he was saying. But his words reflect a common human error: the shortsightedness that mistakes the glory, the wonder, the joy, the inspiration, the pleasure, or the simple comforts of the way station for the journey's end. Jesus knew better. Yes, it would have been wonderful to dig in and take up permanent residence on that marvelous mountaintop, to spend long, leisurely days conferring with Moses and Elijah, discussing the ineffable delights of the life above. But it was not to be. Moses and Elijah had come for only one purpose: to urge the Messiah to go forward until he consummated "his departure, which he was about to bring to fulfillment at Jerusalem." To stay on the mountain would have been to let the world go to ruin around him.

Frodo faced a similar decision. And he chose to leave the safety of the Last Homely House behind.

⤳ *Reflection*

WAY STATIONS ARE IMPORTANT, BUT THEY SHOULD NEVER BE MISTAKEN FOR THE JOURNEY'S END.

LOYAL COMPANION

"So all my plan is spoilt! . . . It is no good trying to escape you. But I'm glad, Sam. I cannot tell you how glad."
(Frodo to Sam—Book II, Chapter 10)

Gandalf was gone. Days earlier he had fallen into a dark chasm while protecting the company from the mighty and terrifying Balrog.

Frodo's protector, the noble Boromir, could no longer be trusted, having been consumed with lust for the power of the One Ring.

His hobbit friends were frightened, yearning for the safety and comforts of their home in the Shire.

The greatest danger still ahead, his wise defender out of the picture, and the evil of the Ring influencing others, Frodo knew what he must do. He had no choice but to continue the quest to which he had been called. And he must continue alone. Those he could trust were too dear to endanger further. So, pushing through the fear that gripped his heart, Frodo hid from his companions in order to sneak off on his own.

The company searched frantically for Frodo, most of all Sam. As Frodo's friend from childhood, Sam Gamgee had shown a touching devotion and admiration for the Ring-bearer that made him a better companion than either had anticipated at the start of their adventure. The only reason Sam was even on the journey was that Gandalf had "punished" his curiosity by sending him along. Since that day, they had been through many joyous and frightening experiences together.

This wasn't the first time Mr. Frodo considered leaving Sam and the others behind. But it wouldn't do. Sam simply could not allow his master to take such a treacherous journey alone, then or now. So he ran as fast as his short legs would carry him down to the river to intercept Frodo, whose resistance was futile. Sam was determined to remain by his master's side. And so, off they went, two simple little hobbits floating downstream away from the safety of numbers and toward the ominous shadows of an evil domain. Regardless of what dangers lay ahead, they were going to face them together, a fact that brought great comfort and encouragement to both.

⊰ ✝ ⊱

Friend. Husband. Wife. Mother. Father. Son. Daughter. Brother. Sister. Partner. Confidante. Mentor. What wonderful words, each suggesting the warmth of acceptance and support, a shoulder to cry on when sad or a friend to celebrate with when happy. Someone to remember your birthday or care about the details of your workday. We were not made to bear the burden and experience the joys of life's journey alone. That's why God has given us the gift of companionship.

The Scriptures talk of a friend who sticks closer than a brother. Such was Sam to Frodo. We do not know whether Frodo would have completed his mission and returned to the Shire had it not been for the faithful companionship of Sam Gamgee. What we do know is that his burden would have been much harder to bear.

> *Two are better than one, because they have a good return*
> *for their work: If one falls down, his friend can help him*
> *up. But pity the man who falls and has no one to help him*
> *up! Also, if two lie down together, they will keep warm.*
> *But how can one keep warm alone? Though one may be*
> *overpowered, two can defend themselves. A cord of three*
> *strands is not quickly broken. (Ecclesiastes 4:9-12)*

Adam was given Eve. God saw that it was not good for the man to be alone. So, taking the rib of one, he formed another. The two, in turn, became one. Each was a gift to the other as a companion on the adventure of life, to love, honor, cherish, and obey for as long as they both lived.

David was given Jonathan. Chosen by God and anointed king of Israel, David would sit upon the throne that legally belonged to Jonathan upon the death of his father, Saul. Jonathan had every reason to hate David. But Jonathan accepted God's choice. He loved David and placed his own life on the line in defense of his friend. Who knows what might have happened to David if not for the loyal companionship of Jonathan?

Moses was given the voice and support of his brother Aaron when called to confront the most powerful man in the world. While awaiting trial, Paul had the steadfast presence of Luke when all others had abandoned him. These and other great leaders accomplished much, but they might have been less successful had it not been for their God-given companions.

Frodo Baggins was given Sam, a fellow hobbit who was not particularly bright or brave. He did not have the wisdom of Gandalf, the courage of Gimli, or the instincts of Strider. But he was trustworthy and loyal, and that is just what Frodo needed most.

Whom have you been given? Who knows just what to say when you're ready to throw in the towel and what not to say when you need silence? Who is it that you call first with the good news because you know they will share your excitement? Who are the ones God has placed in your life to share the burden and the joys of your quest? Don't take these people for granted. They are gifts to be cherished.

~ *Reflection*

A FAITHFUL COMPANION ON THE JOURNEY OF LIFE IS ONE OF GOD'S GREATEST GIFTS.

OFT OVERLOOKED

"We always seem to have got left out of the old lists, and the old stories."
(Merry to Treebeard—Book III, Chapter 4)

It is one thing to be small. It is quite another to be completely overlooked, an unhappy yet frequent experience for Merry, Pippin, and others of their kind. Of course, there were some advantages to obscurity. The folk of Hobbiton had been mostly left to themselves to enjoy the simple pleasures of life in the Shire. Other than Gandalf, none of the Wise paid them any heed. Tales of rising darkness were the concern of others, as Sauron considered hobbits harmless to his aim. Still, benefits aside, even tiny people take pride in their history and character and do not appreciate being disregarded as if their existence were of no consequence whatsoever.

Outside the Shire, the old lists did not contain any references to hobbits. If named at all, they were called "halflings," a less-than-flattering reference at best. Despite a long and rather fascinating story of their own, hobbits were for the most part ignored by the other inhabitants of Middle-earth. But one day all of that changed.

It began when Bilbo Baggins was summoned to adventure by Gandalf, propelling him and others of his race into a great story. Having obtained the One Ring, they knew obscurity was no longer possible. The once secluded hobbits were now objects of great interest, especially to the Dark Lord of Mordor.

"To tell you the truth," replied Gandalf, "I believe that hitherto—hitherto, mark you—he has entirely overlooked the existence of hobbits. You should be thankful. But your safety has passed."[12]

Though small and simple folk, the hobbits had been chosen to fulfill a great purpose. Their innocent and benevolent nature was a key qualification for the task at hand. Frodo and his friends were being called to a quest that could not be accomplished through mere strength or wisdom. It required attributes untarnished by the allure of glory and fame.

Elrond described the task of Frodo as "one that may be attempted by the weak with as much hope as the strong." The weak, he knew, were not tempted by might. Frodo's restraint with the Ring qualified him to be its bearer. As Faramir observed, "I marvel at you: to keep it hid and not use it. You are a new people and a new world to me. Are all your kin of like sort? Your land must be a realm of peace and content, and there must gardeners be in high honour."[13]

And so, in a wonderful twist of irony, the greatest task is given to the smallest people, and the nameless are called to protect the renowned.

⊰ ✛ ⊱

Abraham was an aging nomad with no hope of having children. God chose him to father a great nation.

Joseph was an obnoxious, spoiled brat. God used him to save the world from starvation.

Moses stuttered when he got nervous. He became God's instrument to deliver millions of people and to receive the Ten Commandments.

David was a slingshot-toting kid tending sheep on the hillside. God made him a giant-killer and a grand king.

The twelve disciples were a ragtag bunch. But Jesus invited them to follow him and used them to change the world.

The stories go on and on. It is one of the great ironies of Christian faith. For some reason, God chooses those we least expect to accomplish his most important tasks. Some, like our hobbit friends, emerge from total obscurity to great fame. Others remain anonymous. All are used in ways they never imagined possible. And here is the mystery: They are chosen not in spite of weakness, but because of it.

To some, like the apostle Paul, a weakness must be given to offset the liability of strength. Among the best and brightest of his generation, Paul was highly qualified for success. "If anyone else thinks he has reasons to put confidence in the flesh, I have more," he told the church at Philippi, "circumcised on the eighth day, of the people of Israel, of the tribe of Benjamin, a Hebrew of Hebrews; in regard to the law, a Pharisee . . . as for legalistic righteousness, faultless." But, as he later learned, these strengths were in the way of his usefulness: "But whatever was to my profit I now consider loss for the sake of Christ" (Philippians 3:4-7).

Struck with blindness, Paul began his faith adventure in dependence upon others. He spent the rest of his ministry hampered by what he described as a thorn in the flesh, a constant reminder that God desires our reliance, not our competence. Certainly, he can and will use the latter. But first we must recognize with Paul that "when I am weak, then I am strong" (2 Corinthians 12:10).

Do you remember what happened when Samuel went to the house of Jesse to anoint the next king of Israel? Certain that God wanted to use the strongest leader, Samuel chose the striking Eliab because he demonstrated the qualities of royalty. But God said, "Do not consider his appearance or his height, for I have rejected him. The LORD does not look at the things man looks at. Man looks at the outward appearance, but the LORD looks at the heart" (1 Samuel 16:7).

Then whom does God choose? Whom does he call to fulfill his great purposes? In short, he calls the simple and the weak.

> *Brothers, think of what you were when you were called. Not many of you were wise by human standards; not many were influential; not many were of noble birth. But God chose the foolish things of the world to shame the wise; God chose the weak things of the world to shame the strong. He chose the lowly things of this world and the despised things—and the things that are not—to nullify the things that are, so that no one may boast before him. (1 Corinthians 1:26-29)*

✑ Reflection
GOD OFTEN USES THOSE WE LEAST EXPECT
TO ACCOMPLISH HIS GREATEST WORKS.

NO SAFETY

✛ "If we stayed at home and did nothing,
doom would find us anyway, sooner or later."
(*Treebeard—Book III, Chapter 4*)

Merry and Pippin had been through quite an ordeal.
Separated from their company while searching for Frodo,
the pair was taken captive by a band of repulsive orcs. If it
weren't for a surprise skirmish that distracted their captors,
the two might not have escaped. Fortunately, they were able
to flee into the forest of Fangorn, where they encountered
the strangest creature they had ever seen, an Ent named
Treebeard.

Ents were fourteen feet tall. They appeared to be a cross
between men and trees. Though once a larger population
had roamed the vast regions of Middle-earth, few Ents
remained by the Third Age. Treebeard was still able to walk
and talk, but most had become "treeish," ceasing to move or
speak. Guardian of Fangorn, Treebeard was also one of the
oldest living beings in Middle-earth. Speaking as one with
wisdom only obtained through long life, Treebeard knew the
songs sung since the dawn of time and seemed to understand the story of which each told a part.

The hobbits had never seen an Ent. Nor had Treebeard
seen a hobbit. Neither had known of the other race, causing
a brief period of suspicious caution. But friendship was
sparked when they discovered that both had been in the
company of Gandalf. Before long, Merry and Pippin were
sharing details of their own tale, including a report of

Gandalf's demise. Asking Treebeard whether his race was part of the battle for good, they learned that Ents, like hobbits, tended to keep to themselves.

The hobbits joined Treebeard on his journey to the assembly of Ents. Long harassed by the orc-servants of Saruman, they were finally gathering to decide what to do in response. After a long discussion in a language neither hobbit understood, the Ents decided to march south and attack the fortress of Saruman.

Traveling with the great army of Ents, Merry and Pippin noticed Treebeard's sober demeanor. His eyes were sad, though not unhappy, as one who sensed the coming battle would fulfill a great purpose, but at great cost. They listened to their giant friend reflect upon the equal possibility of victory or defeat. Treebeard knew that the Ents might be heading to their doom. But to seek sanctuary in the forest was greater folly. The evil plans of Saruman no longer allowed them the luxury of idleness. So, come what may, it was time to join the fight!

⊰ ✝ ⊱

Schoolyard bullies start by picking on the small, unpopular kids. Others watch from afar, glad that it's someone else being victimized. What they fail to realize is that their cowardly reluctance to defend the weakest kids will eventually bring about their own jeopardy. Total playground intimidation is inevitable once the bully learns that he faces no opposition. Before you know it, every child will be terrorized.

The history of humankind demonstrates that complacency and appeasement by the decent encourage mischief by the sinister. Only the active, intentional influence of good can counter the progressive nature of bad. And when evil advances, there is no safe haven for the passive.

The world of hobbits was a peaceful, happy place. But Frodo and his companions could not remain comfortably idle, shutting their ears to tales of rising danger. "The wide world is all about you," Gildor told them. "You can fence yourselves in, but you cannot for ever fence it out."[14] Nor could Treebeard and his kind continue hiding in the decreasing protection of Fangorn Forest. Evil was advancing, requiring the active opposition of good.

In the biblical story of Esther, a heinous plot was advancing, requiring heroic risk. Hearing about the impending murder of her people, Queen Esther faced the difficult choice between speaking up on behalf of the Jews or quietly preserving her own life. On penalty of death, she was not allowed to enter the king's presence unless summoned. If she simply remained silent, she might have remained safe. But if she approached the king to plead for intervention, he could order her death along with the masses. Faced with her moment of truth, a frightened young girl received word from her cousin Mordecai.

> Do not think that because you are in the king's house you alone of all the Jews will escape. For if you remain silent at this time, relief and deliverance for the Jews will arise from another place, but you and your father's family will perish. And who knows but that you have come to royal position for such a time as this? (Esther 4:13-14)

Mordecai didn't want Esther to intervene because he thought she was the only hope of rescue for her people. He said, *If you remain silent at this time, relief and deliverance for the Jews will arise from another place.* Mordecai knew that God had a great plan for the Jewish people, making complete annihilation impossible. *But you and your father's family will perish.* He also knew that Esther's own safety was linked to her present choice. *And who knows but that you have come to royal position for such a time as this?* She had been called to play a part in the story, one she could not fulfill by remaining silent. Evil was advancing, making even the palace walls no fortress. And so, heeding her uncle's admonition, Esther risked her own life to save others.

> *I will go to the king, even though it is against the law. And if I perish, I perish. (Esther 4:16)*

Like Esther, Frodo, and Treebeard, we have a choice. We can seek our own safety and comfort by turning a deaf ear to the cries of the weak and shielding our eyes from approaching danger. Or we can use our influence for good, entering the fray to join the active resistance of evil. We are called to nothing less. And if we perish, we perish!

ᕟ Reflection
ONLY THE ACTIVE INFLUENCE OF GOOD CAN
COUNTER THE ADVANCE OF EVIL.

MYSTERIOUS LIGHT

"That we should try to destroy the Ring itself
has not yet entered into his darkest dream."
(Gandalf to the Company—Book III, Chapter 5)

For Aragorn, Legolas, and Gimli it was, in the words of
Dickens, the best of times and the worst of times.

In the forest of Fangorn they had met with unexpected
good fortune. Gandalf was back. Out of the abyss of Moria,
out of fire and darkness and labor and unspeakable anguish,
he had returned. And he was changed, marvelously changed.
Gandalf the Grey had become Gandalf the White. Mith-
randir. The White Rider. A fell and fitting opponent for the
Nine who rode abroad in the service of the Dark Lord. Following such a leader, elves, men, dwarves, and hobbits
might advance against the Shadow with fresh courage and
hope.

But the Shadow was growing, casting a pall across the joy
of their reunion. And the Ring-bearer was moving directly
into its black heart, beyond the help or control of the White
Rider and his companions. The fate of the whole world now
hung in the balance. And no one, not even the mighty Mith-
randir, could tell what the outcome might be.

"Hope is not victory," Gandalf told them. "War is upon
us . . . war in which only the use of the Ring could give us
surety of victory." They all knew that he spoke the truth.

The one surety of victory. And they had sent it away.
Intentionally. Such had been their purpose and plan from the
beginning. The Ring *had* to be destroyed, for its power was

alluring and deceptive and would eventually cause the corruption and downfall of any who sought to wield it.

It was a strategy as mad and uncertain as it was imperative and inevitable. But it did have one great advantage: The Enemy would never expect it.

"He supposes that we were all going to Minas Tirith," Gandalf surmised. "And according to his wisdom it would have been a heavy stroke against his power. . . . That we should try to destroy the Ring itself has not yet entered into his darkest dream."

How could such a thought ever have suggested itself to the mind of Sauron? That anyone should have such power within his grasp and decline to use it—*that*, to a soul so completely darkened by the desire for self-aggrandizement, was absolutely inconceivable.

⊰ ✝ ⊱

Who Wants to Be a Millionaire? It's not just the title of a popular television game show (at the time of this writing, the *most* popular ever conceived). It's a question that goes to the heart of our culture's value system, a probe that touches many of us at the very core of our lives. Who *wouldn't* want to be a millionaire?

"What will you do with the million dollars if you win?" asks the smiling host. "Pay off my school loans," answers the nervous contestant. Others say they'll buy a home; put their kids through college; support their favorite charities.

And as viewers, we nod in agreement because there is so much that can be done with a million dollars. So much good. A million dollars is power in the hand of the person who possesses it. Power to do whatever he or she wants to do. Why would anybody turn down an opportunity like that?

Who wouldn't take the world if it were offered to him? Interestingly enough, the man who had the greatest claim to it, who could have done the most good with it, *didn't*.

> *Again, the devil took him to a very high mountain and showed him all the kingdoms of the world and their splendor. "All this I will give you," he said, "if you will bow down and worship me." Jesus said to him, "Away from me, Satan! For it is written: 'Worship the LORD your God, and serve him only.'"* (Matthew 4:8-10)

In his epistle to the Philippians, Paul pens what might be considered the perfect commentary upon this episode in the life of Jesus:

> *Your attitude should be the same as that of Christ Jesus: Who, being in very nature God, did not consider equality with God something to be grasped, but made himself nothing, taking the very nature of a servant, being made in human likeness. And being found in appearance as a man, he humbled himself and became obedient to death—even death on a cross!* (Philippians 2:5-8)

Why didn't Jesus take the world when it was presented to him on a silver platter? Why, though the Creeds affirm that he was *very God of very God,* did he conclude that divinity, along with the infinite power and potential that go with it, was not something to be "grasped"? When opportunity came knocking, why didn't he get up and open the door?

To those of us who have been tutored in the tenets of the Christian faith, the answer seems obvious. In the first place, Jesus *couldn't* accept any offer that came to him from the hand of Satan. That in itself made the option unthinkable. In the second place, we can see in retrospect that Christ had come to earth on a very different mission: not to seize sovereignty, but to suffer and die.

But those who are less accustomed to traditional Christian doctrine might object that this last point begs a fundamental question. Why death on a cross? Why was this the only road to the goal Jesus sought? Was that really the best, most efficient use of his time and energy? Why not seize the sword when it was held out to him? Why not cut to the chase?

Several characters walk through the wide lands of Middle-earth asking the very same questions. "Why not?" whispers Saruman to Gandalf. "The Ruling Ring? If we could command that, then the Power would pass to *us.*"

"I do not understand all this," objects Boromir at the Council of Elrond. "Why should we not think that the Great Ring has come into our hands to serve us in the very hour of need?"

"At this hour," says Boromir's father, Denethor, Steward of Gondor, "to send [the Ring] in the hands of a witless halfling into the land of the Enemy himself, as you have done . . . that is madness."

Gollum too, in his own mean and small way, ponders what could be done with the limitless power of the Ring: "If we has it, then we can escape, even from Him, eh? Perhaps we grows very strong, stronger than Wraiths. Lord Sméagol? Gollum the Great? *The* Gollum! Eat fish every day, three times a day, fresh from the sea."

The Lady Galadriel, too, imagines an alternate path. "For many long years I had pondered what I might do, should the Great Ring come into my hands. . . . And now at last it comes. You will give me the Ring freely! In place of the Dark

Lord you will set up a Queen. And I shall not be dark, but beautiful and terrible as the Morning and the Night!"

But Galadriel, like Gandalf and like Jesus himself, ultimately resists the temptation. Why? Because Tolkien's Ring, like the devil's offer, is both thoroughly evil and perilously powerful. It is, after all, the One Ring, the single, tiny point at which the potential for universal dominion, the ability to do *whatever one wants to do,* has been localized. And therein, as the wise know very well, lies the seed of evil itself—the same evil that has infected the world since the beginning of human history.

Christ chose a very different path. He did not "grasp." He chose instead to lean upon another. He let great opportunity pass him by. He was "obedient, even to death on a cross." And in so doing, he kindled a light great enough to banish the darkness.

That light, as Gandalf asserted, is a profound mystery to the evil mind. The great Red Eye has no capacity to perceive it.

> For what do righteousness and wickedness have in common? Or what fellowship can light have with darkness? (2 Corinthians 6:14)

> The light shines in the darkness, but the darkness has not understood it. (John 1:5)

That's why Sauron never even saw it coming. Neither did Satan. But for those of us who believe, it is different; for we, in the words of the apostle, "have the mind of Christ" (1 Corinthians 2:16).

➪ Reflection
AN EVIL HEART IS MYSTIFIED BY THE WAYS OF GOOD.

UNWHOLESOME POWER

"Malice eats it like a canker, and the evil is growing."
(Faramir to Frodo—Book IV, Chapter 6)

Frodo and Sam had discovered an unexpected friend and ally. Faramir, captain of Gondor, son of Denethor, and brother to the slain Boromir, had come upon the hobbits while on patrol in the woods of Ithilien. In the cave of Henneth Annûn, stronghold of the men of Gondor, they held long conversation together, and many revelations were made on both sides.

It was while they were there that Sméagol turned up again after a suspicious absence. They caught him lurking at the edge of the Forbidden Pool that lay darkly outside the cave. Faramir's men seized him immediately and returned him to Frodo's custody.

Now it was time to leave this place of safety and take up the desperate quest once more. Frodo intended to resume his arrangement with Sméagol, who had been serving as their guide. But Faramir, understanding that Gollum meant to lead the halflings through the dark and loathsome pass of Cirith Ungol, was afraid to let them continue in his company. "He is wicked," said the Captain. "He will lead you to no good."

That, of course, had been Sam's opinion all along. He didn't trust the wretched creature any further than he could throw him. How could he? He thought back to that night in the Dead Marshes when he woke to discover the "two

Gollums," Slinker and Stinker as Sam had dubbed them, locked in fearful debate over the sleeping form of the Ring-bearer. Gollum was arguing . . . with himself. And the outcome hung in the balance.

> *"Sméagol promised to help the master . . .," Sam heard "Slinker" whine. "Must have it!" hissed "Stinker" in reply, his long-fingered hand slowly extending itself towards Frodo's neck. "We wants it, we wants it, we wants it!"*

There was no telling what might have happened if Sam hadn't interrupted with an exaggerated yawn. He knew that the Ring still had a terrible hold on Sméagol, a hold that almost could not be broken. And he was afraid of what that might mean.

Frodo knew it, too, of course. Hadn't he told Faramir that Gollum was lured to the Forbidden Pool "by a mastering desire, stronger than his caution"? Frodo had seen the effects of that "mastering desire." He knew very well that this thing had completely dominated poor Sméagol, that it had become his very life, stretching him fine and thin, nearly snapping him, depleting him of all feeling except a consuming passion for the "Precious."

Something of the same effect had taken hold even of dear old Bilbo. Even while surrounded by the wholesome influences of Rivendell, Bilbo had not been able to resist the temptation to look upon the Ring once more. Even now the old hobbit was not completely free of its power, and he had borne it for only fifty years or so. How much more formidable was its grip on Gollum, who had possessed the Precious—or been possessed by it—for many long lives of hobbits and men? It was a power to be reckoned with. A power that would not go away.

Frodo stood in the entrance of the cave, picturing poor Sméagol's thin, wizened face. He shuddered. Was *this* what Bilbo—what Frodo himself—might become if the Ring were allowed to have its way?

"Malice eats the creature like a canker," he heard Faramir saying. "And the evil is growing."

⊰ ‡ ⊱

"Each one is tempted," writes the apostle James, "when, by his own evil desire, he is dragged away and enticed. Then, after desire has conceived, it gives birth to sin; and sin, when it is full-grown, gives birth to death" (James 1:14-15).

There is a progressive quality about evil. It begins in the simplest way: with a desire. It begins with a wish to have, to hold, to possess something. And then to use that something to achieve purposes of our own.

The drink. The drug. The other man's wife. Money. Power. Position. There is a sense in which they are nothing to me. It isn't the thing itself, it's what it can do for me that counts. It's the wish for the enhancement and enlargement of self that guides my reaching, grasping hand. The hand needs a tool with which to work its own designs.

It wasn't the fruit that captured the imagination of the first man and woman. It was the attached promise: "You will be like God."

> *When the woman saw that the fruit of the tree was good for food and pleasing to the eye, and also desirable for gaining wisdom, she took some and ate it. She also gave some to her husband, who was with her, and he ate it. (Genesis 3:6)*

And so desire produces action. One thing leads to another. I reach and stretch. I grasp. I lay hold of the object of my desire. And the spinning of a horrible wheel is set in motion. The effect is almost immediate. And it manifests itself—surprise!—not in the enhancement, but in the diminishing of the self.

> Then the eyes of both of them were opened, and they realized they were naked; so they sewed fig leaves together and made coverings for themselves. Then the man and his wife heard the sound of the LORD God as he was walking in the garden in the cool of the day, and they hid from the LORD God among the trees of the garden. (Genesis 3:7-8)

My hand touches the desired object. My fingers close around it. But even as the thrill of possession courses up my arm and through my body, there is a sound from behind me, like the turning of a key in a lock. Already the object has grown and I have begun to decrease. I am trapped within the realization that it's not enough. That I am not more but less than I was, and far less than I ought to be. Sudden fear rears its ugly head. I run for cover, seek a hiding place. In desperation I reach out and grasp again, for more. And the screw is given another turn.

That's how it happened with Sméagol. The bright thing his friend Déagol discovered among the river reeds was a pretty bauble, nothing more. It pleased him and he wanted it. Once he saw it, he knew he *had* to have it. And it was rightfully his, wasn't it? After all, it *was* his birthday! So he killed his companion and fled with the terrible prize. He hid in the dark and followed lightless roads down into the cold cellar of the world, beneath the very roots of the mountains. There he lurked, living a life that was a kind of self-leeching, self-perpetuating misery, clutching the precious birthday present until it made him a ghostlike servant of its own indomitable power.

And so, in the end, the tables are turned. The thing I desired to possess possesses me. Ask the former stockbroker who waits in line at the Skid Row soup kitchen. *He* knows the story of Sméagol from the inside out. He'll tell you that's how he got there. So will the widowed mother of three who stood by and grieved while her handsome young husband—a successful accountant, wonderful father, and highly respected elder in the church—was destroyed, step by slow step, through his growing enslavement to pornography. Or the gambler who has nothing left but bitter memories of loved ones who never want to see his face again. Ask him. He'll tell you that the power he sought to harness for his own purposes somehow got away from him, spinning out of control until it became an unstoppable juggernaut.

If we're not careful, the desire for possession can eat us like a canker. It grows until it fills the entire sky of our personal universe, and the self for which we once cherished such fond hopes ceases to exist.

∽ Reflection
EVIL IS NOT POSSESSED, BUT POSSESSING.

A CROWN OF FLOWERS

"They cannot conquer forever!"
(Frodo to Sam—Book IV, Chapter 7)

It was odd. Though so very near to the wall of Mordor itself—the black, hulking, formless mass of Ephel Dúath, the ill-famed Mountains of Shadow—the woodlands of Ithilien seemed largely untouched by the Threat in the East.

As he and Sam tramped along behind Gollum, Frodo actually found some comfort in stepping over and around the sweet and delicate flowers that dotted the grassy forest glades. The blue and white blossoms of the hyacinths and anemones and the fragile yellow of the celandine awoke in him dim memories of Lórien, Rivendell, and the Shire, places that now felt a world away. After all they had been through, there was something restful about the soft meadows, the cool green shade, the lofty halls, and the bowers they traversed, roofed over with leaves and pillared with the boles of oak and ash trees. These small mementos of goodness and beauty, taken together with the memory of Faramir's friendship and aid, could not help but hearten him. And yet, for all this, he could not escape a sense of brooding, impending doom. The Shadow was growing, and he knew it.

At first it was nothing more than a feeling in the air. The unnatural silence that seemed to deepen with every step. The conspicuous absence of birds and other living creatures. Later it was the stifling closeness, a heaviness in the atmosphere as if a thunderstorm were approaching. When at length they came out from under the trees and into the open, there was no mistaking the source of the oppression. Across the sky, from the darkness in the East to the last fringe of brightness in the West, stretched a spreading, sprawling smudge of twilight and cloud. Slowly but surely, the grasping hand of Mordor was lengthening its reach.

"I'm afraid our journey is drawing to an end," he said to Sam one day when the sun failed to appear. There were rumblings in the earth and in the air and a dull hint of fire in the eastern sky. He had long since resigned himself to this hopeless quest. But now he felt its hopelessness more keenly than ever.

He could not have imagined a more fitting picture of his despair than the one that met his gaze when at last they reached the fatal Cross-roads, the point of departure for the last leg of their grim journey into the Black Land. Far in the West, beyond Minas Tirith and over the sea, the sinking sun dipped below the ragged edge of the spreading darkness and fixed its level beams upon a tall figure of stone, a statue of one of Gondor's ancient kings, seated upon a massive throne. The head had been broken off, cast down, and replaced with a round stone, painted with a toothy grin and a single red eye in the middle of its forehead. The throne and pedestal were covered with rude and obscene scrawls. What an image of nobility and beauty despoiled! It perfectly expressed Frodo's feelings and symbolized the way of the world in these final days of Middle-earth's Third Age.

But then something else caught his eye, something that lay by the roadside in the last light of the sun. It was the statue's head: broken, cracked, and hollow-eyed. But across the stern gray forehead played an incongruous splash of pale color.

"Look, Sam!" cried Frodo. "The king has got a crown again!" And indeed he had. A crown of flowers. A delicate crown of green and silver and gold, the creeping tendrils of a fragile but persistent blossoming plant.

"They cannot conquer forever!" Frodo concluded triumphantly. And the light went out.

❈ ✦ ❈

Dark days have a way of expunging even the memory of the light. Health and hope die easily without constant nourishment, or so it seems, while fear and pessimism, like a mold or a fungus, require only a little thin air and dank dimness to thrive. It isn't long before the "good old days" fade away into the realm of fable or legend: things that never were or will never come again.

It doesn't take much to bring this kind of experience very close to home. Just open up a newspaper or switch on the six o'clock news. *Sixteen Slain in Campus Shooting. Man Admits Shaking Infant to Death. Founder of Christian Charity Convicted in Embezzlement Fraud.* Idealism, once a proud and powerful king, is shattered and knocked from his pedestal. His crown rolls in the dust. Evil wins the day. Cynicism raises its wickedly grinning, one-eyed head and covers our most cherished icons with its filthy graffiti. It becomes easy to believe that the world is nothing but a rude joke.

The prophet Jeremiah complained of this very thing:

> *Why does the way of the wicked prosper? Why do all the faithless live at ease? You have planted them, and they have taken root; they grow and bear fruit. (Jeremiah 12:1-2)*

This same darkness can fall in more immediate and personal ways. It descends as the doctor grimly purses his lips and shakes his head. It drops with a thud, like the final curtain on the last act, as he pronounces the word "malignant" or "terminal." It grows and spreads and reigns in the silence of an icy spouse. It knocks you flat as a teenaged son or daughter flings the words "I hate you!" and slams the door with a flourish. "I've found somebody else," says a distant voice on the other end of the phone; and with Frodo, we sigh and say, "I'm afraid our journey is drawing to an end." It was a good fight while it lasted, but it's all over now. The Shadow has prevailed.

Many Christian believers at the beginning of the third millennium feel as if they have a great deal in common with the Elves at the end of Middle-earth's Third Age. Our world is changing for the worse. Many fair things are passing away; indeed, many are already long gone. The pall of evil is spreading, growing, engulfing everything. The post-Christian era has arrived and established permanent residency. A few islands of sanity and goodness remain, of course, a Rivendell here, a Lothlórien there, but soon they too will be swept away. We kept up a brave front as long as we could, but the eve of our departure is at hand. Let's bar the doors, batten down the hatches, and get out while we can. The end is near.

It's at moments like these that we're arrested by a whisper in our ear. A small voice from behind says, "Sam Gamgee's old Gaffer was right: *where there's life, there's hope.*" We turn our head, glance to one side, and suddenly, in some obscure corner where no one would have expected to find it, we discover fresh new evidence of burgeoning spiritual life— fragile, perhaps; small and tender, but tenacious and unconquerable.

This has been the experience of the church over and over again throughout the long centuries of its history. Just when death seems to have triumphed at last, up through the cracks of the hard, dry earth springs a tender curl of green, crowned with silver and gold. Suddenly we remember: Christ lives. And because he lives, the enemy's defeat is certain. It's just a matter of time.

Like Frodo, the psalmist was enabled to grasp this truth only after traveling a long, hard road:

> When I tried to understand all this [the prosperity of the wicked], it was oppressive to me till I entered the sanctuary of God; then I understood their final destiny. Surely you place them on slippery ground; you cast them down to ruin. How suddenly are they destroyed, completely swept away by terrors! As a dream when one awakes, so when you arise, O LORD, you will despise them as fantasies. (Psalm 73:16-20)

> A little while, and the wicked will be no more; though you look for them, they will not be found. But the meek will inherit the land and enjoy great peace. (Psalm 37:10-11)

British journalist, critic, and essayist Malcolm Muggeridge put it this way:

> Let us then as Christians rejoice that we see around us on every hand the decay of the institutions and instruments of power, see intimations of empires falling to pieces, money in total disarray, dictators and parliamentarians alike nonplused by the confusion and conflicts which encompass them. For it is precisely when every earthly hope has been

> explored and found wanting, when every possibility of
> help from earthly sources has been sought and is not forth-
> coming, when every recourse this world offers, moral as
> well as material, has been explored to no effect, when in
> the shivering cold the last [log] has been thrown on the fire
> and in the gathering darkness every glimmer of light has
> finally flickered out, it's then that Christ's hand reaches
> out sure and firm.[15]

The crown of flowers, though seemingly frail, is an ever-living, everlasting crown, the crown of the King of kings. No wonder the enemy is angry: "He is filled with fury, because he knows that his time is short" (Revelation 12:12).

⤳ Reflection

EVIL MAY PREVAIL FOR A DAY, BUT ITS FINAL
DEFEAT IS CERTAIN.

A GOOD END

"We hear about those as just went on—and
not all to a good end, mind you; at least not
to what folk inside a story and not outside
it call a good end."

(Sam to Frodo—Book IV, Chapter 8)

A conniving Gollum had led Frodo and Sam to a dreadful
place. Hoping to discover an unguarded path into Mordor,
the hobbits instead found themselves climbing the seemingly
endless stairs of Cirith Ungol. Properly translated "Pass of
the Spider," the dark path emitted the foul stench of death.
Spent from their treacherous ascent, Frodo and Sam paused
to refresh themselves with what might be their final meal.
The most perilous duty of their quest was at hand, leaving
no room for hunger or fatigue. So they rested in the shadows
of impending danger.

Sam distrusted Gollum as a guide, convinced he was leading them into enemy hands. It was clear that Gollum wanted
only the Ring and would do anything to possess it again.
The lives of two hobbits would be small payment to regain
his "Precious." But Frodo insisted they follow, persuaded
that this wretched creature might yet play an important part
in their destiny.

While eating, Sam and Frodo considered their situation,
wondering how they had become part of such a grand
adventure when neither had pursued it. In the old stories,
it seemed, the brave folk went out looking for excitement,
as if to escape boredom. But maybe not. Actually, in the best

tales, the hero is required to confront danger he would never willingly seek. In those adventures, ordinary people resist the urge to turn back or hide. They instead summon the courage necessary to overcome fear and face jeopardy.

> "But I expect they had lots of chances, like us, of turning back, only they didn't." Sam reflected. "And if they had, we shouldn't know, because they'd have been forgotten. We hear about those as just went on—and not all to a good end, mind you; at least not to what folk inside a story and not outside it call a good end."

They thought of Mr. Bilbo's tale. His adventure had come to a good end, in which he arrived home unharmed. They hoped for such an ending to their story. "But those aren't always the best tales to hear," recalls Sam, "though they may be the best tales to get landed in!"

Wondering what sort of story they had fallen into, each encouraged the other with thoughts of future days when songs and stories might be written about them. Maybe, if they pressed on in courage, children would someday ask to hear their favorite story, the one about Frodo Baggins with his faithful companion Samwise Gamgee and their quest to destroy the Ring of Doom.

But they also faced the grim possibility that this part of the story, the part where Frodo and Sam approach the Pass of the Spider, would cause frightened children to say with a shudder, "Shut the book now . . . we don't want to read any more."

⊸ ✦ ⊱

As Frodo and Sam realized, our perspective from inside the story is very different from what it would be from the outside. In fact, it is possible that the scenes we would least seek will someday prove to be the best in the tale being told.

Some of our favorite stories are based upon the lives of those who accepted the unexpected call to adventure. Their courage in the face of danger, uncertainty, or distress inspires our hearts. And, more often than not, our favorite part of their story is a scene they would have never willingly pursued.

Joseph did not want to be thrown into a hole by his jealous brothers. Nor did he enjoy being sold into slavery or falsely accused and imprisoned by Potiphar. These and other scenes make his a part one would not choose to play. But each situation also became an opportunity for Joseph to fulfill a heroic role in the drama of faith. He summoned the courage to trust a God Joseph believed to be good despite contrary evidence of personal tragedy. Only after years of injustice and suffering did he see how the scenes of life he most hated were those most important to the story being told. "Am I in the place of God?" he asked those who had caused him harm. "God intended it for good to accomplish what is now being done, the saving of many lives" (Genesis 50:19-20).

Three Hebrew young men were placed in a scene they did not pursue. Despite being deported from their homeland, Shadrach, Meshach, and Abednego were determined to obey God's command, "Do not bow to any graven image." But their pagan king had other ideas, demanding that they worship a statue of himself. On threat of being burned alive in a blazing furnace, they stood their ground. Eye to eye with the man who could order their execution, they found courage.

> If we are thrown into the blazing furnace, the God we serve is able to save us from it, and he will rescue us from your hand, O king. (Daniel 3:17)

But they had no reason to expect him to do so. After all, God had not prevented their deportation or rescued them from forced service in the court of an arrogant tyrant. In fact, it had been generations since the last reported miracle. They had no more reason to expect miraculous intervention than you or I do today. And so, showing the true depth of their bravery, they added these words:

> But even if he does not, we want you to know, O king, that we will not serve your gods or worship the image of gold you have set up. (Daniel 3:18)

"But even if he does not . . ." Potent words. Amazing courage. These three were determined that theirs would be an adventure with a good end, no matter what came. If they were rescued, theirs would be a tale of joy, with everyone living happily ever after. But if not, it would be a tale of courage, the kind children ask their fathers to tell and retell. They understood that the big drama is about more than comfort and safety. It is about whether ordinary men and women can stubbornly cling to their faith no matter what the scenes of life may bring.

You and I live our lives on that same stage. But God exists on and offstage, viewing the entire spectrum of creation and history from outside, beyond, above. And it is his perspective of the story, not ours, that defines "a good end."

> Blessed is the man who perseveres under trial, because when he has stood the test, he will receive the crown of life that God has promised to those who love him. (James 1:12)

Reflection

OFTEN THE SCENES WE LEAST DESIRE ARE THOSE MOST IMPORTANT TO THE STORY BEING TOLD.

SINGING IN THE DARK

> And then softly, to his own surprise, there at the vain end of his long journey and his grief, moved by what thought in his heart he could not tell, Sam began to sing.
>
> (Book VI, Chapter 1)

It had happened at last. The very worst thing Sam could imagine.

Mr. Frodo—dead! Killed by the giant spider Shelob! There he lay on the floor of the loathsome monster's lair, still, pale, and deathly cold.

Sam had fought the great spider heroically. He had even dealt her a deadly wound. But Sam had come too late. And now, try as he might, he could not rouse Frodo. He cut the thick, ropy strands of web that bound his master, kissed his cold forehead, and chafed his limp hands. But it was useless.

Tears welled up in Sam's eyes. After all they'd been through together! The Ring-bearer was dead, and the Quest had failed. All hope was gone. Unless . . . unless Sam could summon up the courage to see it through alone. Only for a moment did he hesitate. Then, taking the Ring from Frodo's motionless body, he set out.

That was when the worst got worse. Orcs! They stumbled upon Frodo and carried him off! Making use of the Ring, Sam followed them invisibly; and in overhearing their harsh talk, he made a discovery that took his breath away: Frodo was *not* dead after all, just stunned with the spider's venom. Sam's face burned hot with shame and rage. His master was alive and captured by the enemy! There was only one thing to do: follow the orcs to the Tower of Cirith Ungol and rescue him . . . or die trying.

Darkness, death, and terror surrounded him as he approached the brazen gates and slipped inside with the help of Galadriel's lamp. Up the endless steps he made his way. Near the top he was forced to fight. Then, his enemy repulsed for the moment, he leapt up the stairs once more until he came to a dead end.

Now what? Gasping for breath and sick with despair, Sam sat down on the steps. What else could he do? He expected his enemy to return at any moment. *Well,* he thought, *the end has come at last.* The guttering torch on the wall flickered and went out. Sam put his head in his hands.

And then, without knowing why, there in the darkness and gloom, he started to sing. He sang softly and with a bit of trembling at first; then louder and with growing confidence as his spirits inexplicably rose. And suddenly he thought he heard a faint voice trying to sing in reply.

"Ho la! You up there, you dunghill rat!" called the orc who was guarding Frodo. "Stop your squeaking or I'll come and deal with you!"

Sam jumped to his feet. No longer were orc-danger and the possibility of discovery of any importance to him. The song and the singing had led him to his master!

⊰ ✝ ⊱

"On Christmas night all Christians sing," declares an old carol. In a certain sense, these six words represent the sum total of Christian experience. "In the bleak midwinter," at the very darkest season of the year, faithful voices around the world rise in praise to the dawning of the everlasting light. Nor is that the only time the church lifts its collective voice in song.

From the very beginning, singing has been one of the distinguishing trademarks of those who go on Christian pilgrimage. One might almost go so far as to say that singing is a distinctively Christian activity. Other faith-traditions have their music, of course: canticles, chanted prayers, liturgical verses. But followers of Jesus *sing*: loud and long, jubilantly, triumphantly, even raucously. And they do it in the most unlikely situations.

Consider Paul and Silas in the Philippian jail. They'd had a hard day, even by apostolic standards. First there was the spiritual confrontation with the demon-possessed slave girl. Then the angry shouts of her owners once they realized their livelihood was gone. Then the uproar in the marketplace, the kicks and blows, the rough escort into the presence of the Roman magistrates, the flying accusations. At last, to top it all off, they had been stripped, beaten with rods, and thrown into the local jail. All in a day's work, perhaps, but painful and exhausting nonetheless.

There they sat, chained to the wall, hands and feet bound in the stocks, strips of flesh hanging from their raw, bleeding backs. Darkness fell. And then the strangest thing happened. Near midnight, at the blackest hour, Paul and Silas began to sing.

> *About midnight Paul and Silas were praying and singing hymns to God. . . . Suddenly there was such a violent earthquake that the foundations of the prison were shaken. At once all the prison doors flew open, and everybody's chains came loose. . . . The jailer called for lights, rushed*

> *in and fell trembling before Paul and Silas. He then*
> *brought them out and asked, "Sirs, what must I do to be*
> *saved?" (Acts 16:25-30)*

Songs in the night. The prophet Isaiah had spoken of them six hundred years earlier (Isaiah 30:29). The apostles must have heard his words read many times. Somehow the phrases came back to them in their hour of need. And so they sang. And as they lifted their voices, the wheels of the world were moved, a man and his household were saved, and history was changed.

In the same way, a song came to Sam when he needed it most. The plot turned and events were redirected as he sang. It was a crucial moment in the history of the Quest of the Ring. And it found definition through the power of song.

Song is central to the history of Tolkien's Middle-earth. The tale of *The Lord of the Rings* is constantly punctuated with singing. Tom Bombadil sings as he rescues the hobbits from danger. Aragorn sings of Beren and Lúthien upon the dark and dangerous heights of Weathertop. Legolas sings of the wanderings of Nimrodel beside the stream that bears the elven-maiden's name. Treebeard gives Merry and Pippin the tale of the Ents and the Entwives in song. Faramir and the Lady Éowyn stand upon the walls of Gondor and hear a great eagle singing of the return of the king and the defeat of Sauron. Bilbo ties the entire epic together with his song of the road that "goes ever on and on."

But Sam's song in the tower of Cirith Ungol is perhaps the best and most representative of them all. It's a song that celebrates the believer's faith in a Larger Reality—a reality that rolls on unceasingly, above and beyond the present hour of darkness:

Though here at journey's end I lie
in darkness buried deep,
beyond all towers strong and high,
beyond all mountains steep,
above all shadows rides the Sun
and Stars for ever dwell:
I will not say the Day is done,
nor bid the Stars farewell.

An old Quaker hymn expresses the same thought in different words:

What though the tempest round me roars?
I know the Truth, it liveth;
What though the darkness round me blows?
Songs in the night it giveth.
No storm can shake my inmost calm
While to that Rock I'm clinging.
Since Love is Lord of heaven and earth,
How can I keep from singing?

Reflection

IT IS NEVER SO DARK THAT WE CANNOT SING.

UNWITTING INSTRUMENT

✢ "But do you remember Gandalf's words:
Even Gollum may have something yet to do"?
(Frodo to Sam—Book VI, Chapter 3)

The quest was achieved! Sam and Frodo, sitting upon the dark mountain, were overcome with wearied joy. The Ring had been destroyed, consumed in the flames of the Cracks of Doom. Starving and thirsty, with little hope of their own rescue, both delighted in a triumphant end to their adventure.

Neither hobbit could have imagined the events that would have to transpire to bring success. Only a few days earlier they had stood at the foot of Mount Doom, its foreboding trail demanding more strength than either possessed. But there had been no choice in the matter; they knew they simply must reach the peak. Weakened by the burden of the Ring, Frodo had to be carried part of the way. But Sam was willing, resolute in his task to stay with his master to the end, even if it meant his own demise. "So that was the job I felt I had to do when I started . . . to help Mr. Frodo to the last step and then die with him? Well, if that is the job then I must do it." Sam's resolve had been tested with times of deep despair. Its hope spent, his spirit longed to give up the journey: "It's all quite useless," he thought. "He said so himself. You are the fool, going on hoping and toiling." But he resisted the temptation to quit, determined to serve Mr. Frodo to the end.

As it turned out, Sam did not have to die. Moments before

they reached the fire, calamity was averted through the mysterious convergence of two wicked purposes. First, placing the
Ring on his finger, Frodo vanished before Sam's eyes. Possessing its bearer, the Ring seemed to be defending itself. "I
will not do this deed," Frodo proclaimed. "The Ring is mine!"
Evil had taken control of the Ring-bearer in hopes of prevent-
ing its own ruin. Suddenly, the eye of the Dark Lord was
aware, placing the hobbits' quest and lives in mortal danger.

Second, a pursuing Gollum violently attacked Sam, causing his head to strike the stony floor. Helpless against the
advance, Sam could only watch from afar as Gollum overtook
Mr. Frodo. Inflamed by the lust for unending life offered by
his "Precious," the miserable fiend determined to regain custody of it. In maddened rage, he bit the bearing finger from
Frodo's hand, releasing the golden prize. But as Gollum
danced about in jubilant conquest, he stepped too far. As if
summoned by its rising flames, the creature and the Ring fell
together over the chasm's edge. Gollum clung tightly to his
Precious as both fell into the depths of destruction.

In order to protect itself from the flames, the Ring overtook Frodo's will. But already enslaved to its powers, Gollum
served an unintended aim. And so, the one willing to die
was delivered through the doom of one chasing immortality.

It was not at all as Sam had pictured. He saw himself a
hero, possibly dying alongside his master, nobly sacrificing
life and limb to free the Shire from the eye of the Dark Lord,
Sauron. He never anticipated that smelly, treacherous Gollum
would play such a part. In fact, Sam had almost killed the
wretched creature. But something had restrained him, as if
Gollum's fate were wed to his own. As it turned out, the two
fates were tied more than he could have known.

"But for him, Sam, I could not have destroyed the Ring,"

came Frodo's haunting words. "The Quest would have been in vain, even at the bitter end." Just as Gandalf had prophesied, Gollum had a part to play, the part of unwitting instrument.

As ancient lore foretold, the counter melody of Melkor's rebellion was used as an unwitting instrument in the hands of a great composer. "For he that attempteth this," the words of Ilúvatar echo, "shall prove but mine instrument in the devising of things more wonderful, which he himself hath not imagined."[16] Gollum had no intention of destroying the Ring. But as fate would have it, he alone was able to assure its demise. Frodo, though willing, was unable to overcome its power. And so, what evil intended, good used.

⊰ ✦ ⊱

Nothing occurs in life that does not ultimately align with God's purposes. Even the distorted schemes of evil can become tools in the hands of providence.

> Oh, the depth of the riches of the wisdom and knowledge of God! How unsearchable his judgments, and his paths beyond tracing out! "Who has known the mind of the Lord? Or who has been his counselor?" "Who has ever given to God, that God should repay him?" For from him and through him and to him are all things. To him be the glory forever! Amen. (Romans 11:33-36)

If it is all from him, through him, and to him, there is no room for the plans of others. In what is the greatest mystery in all of life, God is able to draw all things together to fulfill his great purposes. And one of those purposes is the ultimate good of those whom he has called to sing his song.

> We know that in all things God works for the good of
> those who love him, who have been called according to
> his purpose. (Romans 8:28)

Those purposes also include using the intentions of the
wicked to undermine their own goals and, at the same time,
fulfill his.

> The wicked plot against the righteous and gnash their
> teeth at them; but the LORD laughs at the wicked, for he
> knows their day is coming. The wicked draw the sword
> and bend the bow to bring down the poor and needy, to
> slay those whose ways are upright. But their swords will
> pierce their own hearts, and their bows will be broken.
> (Psalm 37:12-15)

Pharaoh hardened his heart, refusing to let God's people go.
So God used his stubborn pride to tell a story of deliverance.

The Midianites, Amalekites, and other eastern nations
joined forces, assembling a mighty army to crush and dominate Israel. So God placed fear and confusion in their hearts
and had them all kill one another, to the surprise of Gideon
and his three hundred men.

Goliath cursed the Jews and their God, trying to shame
them into a battle they were sure to lose. So God used the
death of a giant to exalt a boy and defeat the Philistines.

Satan leads a chorus of rebellion against the good song of
God. So God calls you and me to sing a righteous melody
and fulfill a grand quest.

Be it the lust of Gollum, the plans of Sauron, or the decep-
tions of Satan, everything that opposes God's story will ultimately serve its plot. And someday, flames similar to those

that destroyed the Ring of Doom will consume another rebellion.

> *The devil, who deceived them, was thrown into the lake of burning sulfur, where the beast and the false prophet had been thrown.* (Revelation 20:10)

⤳ *Reflection*
EVEN EVIL MUST ULTIMATELY SERVE
GOD'S PURPOSES.

KING OF HEARTS

> But when Aragorn arose . . . it seemed
> to them that he was revealed to them
> now for the first time.
> (Book VI, Chapter 5)

The hour had come. Throughout the long years of his life Aragorn had anticipated it, fought for it, and worked toward it with expectancy and determination. Over the far-flung paths and trackless wastes of the wide world he had sought it, ranging from east to west and north to south, always bending his steps toward this one point in time, this one particular spot of ground.

Spring was ripening into summer. The very buds on the greening trees of Gondor seemed ready to burst with joy. It was as if the inhabitants of the city had suddenly awakened from a long nightmare. The One Ring had been destroyed. The Shadow in the East had failed and scattered like smoke on the winds of the morning. And the king was waiting just outside the gate.

Just days earlier, standing upon the walls of Minas Tirith and looking out eastward, Faramir the Steward and Éowyn, Lady of Rohan, had seen a great eagle come winging its way over the city, crying aloud as it flew:

> Sing and be glad, all ye children of the West,
> for your King shall come again,
> and he shall dwell among you
> all the days of your life.

Now, on the field before the gate of Minas Tirith, the striped pavilions of the Lords of the West stood bright in the morning sun. Inside the city, every street, every doorway, every window flowed with garlands of fresh flowers. The gate itself was thronged with men in flashing armor, with women and children in garments of every hue. The music of harps, flutes, and silver horns filled the air.

"Behold!" cried Faramir as Aragorn approached the gate at the head of his kinsmen, the Dúnedain. "One has come to claim the kingship again at last. Shall he be king and enter into the City and dwell there?"

The reply was one of loud and unanimous acclaim. *"Yes!"*

The crown was produced from a black and silver casket. It was made of silver itself, with the wings of a seabird, fashioned of silver and pearl, attached at each side. At Aragorn's request, Frodo bore it to the king and Gandalf placed it upon his head. Another great shout went up. This was the moment they had all been awaiting.

At last Aragorn arose and stood before them, a king indeed. All gazed upon him in silent awe. For it was as if they were seeing him for the first time. He was like a new man, ancient of days, but vigorous, hale, and hearty, a man they had known well and yet had never known before.

"Out of the Great Sea to Middle-earth I am come," he said, reciting the words of his forefather Elendil. "In this place will I abide, and my heirs, unto the ending of the world."

And again the people cheered and shouted and wept tears of joy.

⊰ ☩ ⊱

Picture it. Try to feel how it must feel. There he stands before you, a leader like no leader you've ever imagined.

Mighty in war and wise in counsel. Firm but patient, and
tirelessly compassionate. Not a politician or a mere candi-
date for your support but a figure commanding your loyalty, fealty, and obedience. The embodiment and icon of
everything you hold to be good and true and worthy of
affection. Wouldn't you lay everything aside for his sake?
Wouldn't you, like Ceorl of Rohan, kneel before him,
offer him your notched sword, and cry, "Command me,
lord"?[17]

This ideal king, the long-lost, desperately-wished-for,
someday-to-return king is part of our human heritage.
He is, in fact, essential to our collective identity and self-
understanding as a people. And he plays a leading role in
some of our oldest and most cherished legends.

Consider Arthur. Risen from obscurity, he unites all
of Britain in a reign of unparalleled glory and defines the
very essence of Britishness. Betrayed, he suffers a deadly
wound and passes beyond the realm of human knowledge.
"Yet some men say," writes Sir Thomas Malory, ". . . that
King Arthur is not dead, but had by the will of our Lord
Jesus into another place; and men say that he shall come
again . . . that there is written upon his tomb this verse:
HIC IACET ARTHURUS, REX QUONDAM REX QUE
FUTURUS"—Here lies Arthur, the Once and Future
King.[18]

Similar tales have been told of other beloved monarchs
and leaders. Of Fionn MacCumhail (Finn MacCool), Chief-
tain of the Fianna in Ireland, it was said that he never
truly died but was hidden from human sight in a secret
cavern with his comrades in arms, "where they await the
appointed time to reappear in glory and redeem their land
from tyranny and wrong."[19] Medieval Germans said much

the same thing about King Frederick Barbarossa, one of the earliest and most powerful of the Holy Roman Emperors. For the French it was Charlemagne. Tolkien's Gimli echoes this hope, speaking of the archetypal father of the Dwarves: "O Kheled-zâram fair and wonderful!" he exclaims, gazing at the ring of stars reflected in the Mirrormere. "There lies the crown of Durin till he wakes."[20]

Why this fundamental longing for a king? Why did the Israelites of old complain to Samuel that they did not have one (1 Samuel 8:4-5)? Why, when rebuked and dealt a sore buffet by the disguised Richard Coeur d'Leon in Sherwood Forest, did Robin Hood kneel and confess, "I love no man in all the world so well as I do my King"?

Does all of this sound foreign and archaic to twenty-first-century Americans, with our 250-year-old tradition of independence, self-reliance, and disdain for tyranny? It shouldn't. Doubters need only ponder the significance of a shrine like Graceland. Supermarket tabloids are *still* printing reports that Elvis has been sighted in a Memphis gas station or a Biloxi diner. After nearly half a century, we continue to pine for the return of "The King."

It seems there's no denying it. Like the Jews, we're all waiting expectantly for the arrival of our Messiah: *Mashiach*, the Anointed One, the King who will not disappoint our hopes and dreams like all the others, but fulfill them.

> *My heart is stirred by a noble theme*
> *as I recite my verses for the king;*
> *my tongue is the pen of a skillful writer.*
> *You are the most excellent of men*
> *and your lips have been anointed with grace,*
> *since God has blessed you forever.*

Gird your sword upon your side, O mighty one;
clothe yourself with splendor and majesty.
(Psalm 45:1-3)

Passages like this spring to mind as Tolkien describes the coronation of Aragorn. The power of the scene lies in its appeal to something deep within the psyche of every reader: the wish for a king who is truly worthy of loyalty and worship. When he rises with the crown upon his head, Aragorn is revealed to be just such a king: master and ruler, not only of his people's lands and houses, but of their *hearts*.

To the inhabitants of Gondor he is no longer merely Strider, Ranger of the North. He is now Elessar, Elfstone, Ruler of the West and Lord of many great lords.

As such, he cannot fail to remind us of Jesus, once the humble carpenter of Nazareth, now the rider on the white horse, the Word of God, whose name is Faithful and True.

His eyes are like blazing fire, and on his head are many
crowns. . . . On his robe and on his thigh he has this name
written: KING OF KINGS AND LORD OF LORDS.
(Revelation 19:12, 16)

This is the message that no believer can fail to recall as the eagle soars over Gondor and the people shout for joy. The King *has* come. And the King *will* come again. He is in truth the "Once and Future King," the King of every heart.

☙ *Reflection*

IN OUR HEART OF HEARTS, EACH OF US LONGS
TO SERVE THE TRUE KING.

SEDUCTIVE VOICE

> "Do not believe him! He has lost all power,
> save his voice that can still daunt you
> and deceive you, if you let it."
> (Frodo—Book VI, Chapter 8)

They were deceived. Intimidated by thieving bands of ruffians, few hobbits dared stand against the oppression of one who had come to rule the Shire. Those who did resist found it a solitary effort, unaided by once friendly neighbors either hiding from or serving the new "boss" of Hobbiton.

His name was Sharkey. He had taken up residence at Bag End, once home to Bilbo and Frodo Baggins. From this new fortress he ruled a frightened community, pilfering what he wanted while laying waste the once graceful landscape. Felled trees and shacks had long since replaced forest-bordered cottages, consuming the simple charm of hobbit living in the oppressive reign of Mordor.

Frodo, Sam, Pippin, and Merry returned from adventure to a home much changed. Remembering its former beauty made its ruin an even greater sadness. They now empathized with the grief of Gimli when he gazed longingly upon the remains of a once grand Dwarrowdelf. They understood loss as never before, seeing their lovely haven fallen into ugliness. But sadness did not become despair, for the four knew the present scene to be an empty echo of the former age. The Shire would be made right again once its citizens received the good news of redemption.

Word of the Ring's destruction had not yet reached

Hobbiton, making it an illicit province of ignorance. The boss they feared was nothing more than the hireling of a defeated foe and his ruffians mere thugs requiring confrontation rather than concession. The Dark Tower had fallen, and there was a king in Gondor. Once that truth was known, freedom could again reign in the Shire.

But Sharkey had done more than change the landscape of Bag End; he had manipulated the thinking of its residents. It had been some time since hobbits went about their business without fear of his dominion. They believed his claims and lived accordingly. Regardless of what had transpired beyond the Shire, Sharkey still ruled within it.

The returning hobbits knew what must be done. The boss of Bag End had to be confronted and exposed as a charlatan. Reaching the place Frodo had once called home and finding it now in filthy disrepair, the company was confronted with a familiar form and unwelcome laugh. It was their old foe Saruman, using a new name and gloating over his most recent conquest. Mocking the halflings as inferiors, he claimed power to avenge any abuse. Most of the threatened hobbits recoiled. But Frodo, knowing the truth, refused to be intimidated.

"Do not believe him!" he proclaimed. "He has lost all power, save his voice that can still daunt you and deceive you, if you let it."

In truth, Saruman was impotent. His powers had been consumed along with the Ring in the flames of defeat. But he had one remaining weapon: the low, enchanting voice of which they had been warned at the door of Orthanc. "Beware of his voice," Gandalf had said. Saruman's seductive speech had manipulated the long-freed residents of the Shire, keeping them under his control. He could use his voice to do so again. But only, according to Frodo, if they let him.

⊰ ✝ ⊱

There are two ways to control. The first is tyranny, imposing one's will through force. The second is deception, persuading others to believe a well-told lie. Deception is more common and more effective, as modeled by the one who seeks to make himself the illicit "boss" of our domain. And like Saruman's, his speech is very seductive. "You will not surely die," came his first lie.

> For God knows that when you eat of it your eyes will be opened, and you will be like God, knowing good and evil. (Genesis 3:4-5)

We took the bait, opening our lovely realm to his devilish sway. We invited evil into our once tranquil homeland, and human experience has been dominated by the ruffians of fear, pain, sorrow, and confusion ever since. But the true menace is not these lesser adversaries. If we're abused, we know it. If tempted or oppressed, we know it. But when we're deceived, we don't know it. That's what makes deception such a powerful weapon in the hands of our enemy. Jesus warned of his voice:

> When he lies, he speaks his native language, for he is a liar and the father of lies. (John 8:44)

The lies continue. Though the true King has entered history to reclaim the throne of our hearts, we go on living in bondage, believing "Sharkey" is still in charge. But it need not be so. Yes, he can daunt and deceive, but only if we let him.

> *If you hold to my teaching, you are really my disciples. Then you will know the truth, and the truth will set you free. (John 8:32)*

Truth can be known, for it has been revealed. In the hearts of men as in the hearts of hobbits, freedom is available to anyone willing to believe what is rather than what appears to be.

> *The god of this age has blinded the minds of unbelievers, so that they cannot see the light of the gospel of the glory of Christ. . . . For God, who said, "Let light shine out of darkness," made his light shine in our hearts to give us the light of the knowledge of the glory of God in the face of Christ. (2 Corinthians 4:4-6)*

What we believe to be true has a direct influence upon how we live, whether that belief is actually true or not. The good news of the gospel is redemption. Evil is defeated, the rightful King has reclaimed the throne, and the deceptive reign of darkness is at an end. Freedom is offered to those who are willing to accept the reality that Sharkey's rule is a fraud. That is the way it is, regardless of the way things appear to be.

ᕙ *Reflection*
WE ARE RULED BY WHAT WE BELIEVE,
WHETHER IT'S TRUE OR NOT.

REDEMPTION

"It must often be so, Sam, when things
are in danger: some one has to give them up,
lose them, so that others may keep them."
(Frodo to Sam—Book VI, Chapter 9)

All's well as ends better!" Old Gaffer never spoke so
true.

Sharkey's end opened restoration to the Shire. Having
freed their enslaved and imprisoned neighbors, the heroic
hobbits turned their attention to redeeming their homeland.
Frodo agreed to serve as deputy mayor for a time, restoring
justice and order where tyranny had ruled. Merry and Pippin
took the task of hunting out the last of the ruffians. And
Sam, aided by Galadriel's gift, set upon restoring recklessly
felled trees and the once fertile landscapes.

The Shire had become a better place than before, its
dreadful loss enriching the soil in which a new era could
grow. The folk of Hobbiton were enjoying the deepest hap-
piness they had known, as though the experience of grief
had somehow increased their capacity for joy. Were the trees
really growing taller or were the hobbits simply more aware
of grandeur? Were the colors more vivid or the hobbits' eyes
more attuned to beauty? Were the children born stronger
and more fair or their parents more grateful for the gift of
life? Perhaps it was both. Like recovering a misplaced trea-
sure thought forever gone, the folk of the Shire were drink-
ing deeply from the cup of gladness.

Amid the festivity of restoration, few noticed Mr. Frodo's

gradual withdrawal. None saw his silent suffering, unaware of his lingering illness. But Sam, despite his work and newly married life, took notice, growing more and more concerned for his master and friend. It was bad enough that he, Merry, and Pippin seemed to be receiving more recognition for their adventures than Mr. Frodo. His had been the more important part, both in the Quest and in telling its story. To make matters worse, Sam sensed that his master was becoming increasingly distracted, as if preparing to depart.

> "What's the matter, Mr. Frodo?" said Sam.
> "I am wounded," he answered, "wounded; it will never really heal."

It had been two years that day since Frodo received the terrible wound in the dell under Weathertop.

A new year came, and Mr. Frodo continued to conceal his pain with great effort. Until one day, entering Sam's study with a look of finality, he invited his dear companion to accompany him on another journey. Uncle Bilbo Baggins had reached his 131st birthday, surpassing the Old Took, and the two would travel to celebrate with him. "I wish I could go all the way with you," came Sam's reply. But they knew he could only go part of the way. A new father, Sam knew that long adventures were a completed chapter in his story.

While preparing to go, Sam was presented with the book begun many years earlier. The book, in which Bilbo and Frodo tell tales of the parts the hobbits had played in the downfall of the Lord of the Rings, was now nearly complete. "I have quite finished, Sam," said Frodo. "The last pages are for you." It was now clear to Sam what was happening. Mr. Frodo was finalizing details as he prepared to leave Middle-

earth along with other Ring-bearers. He had received a mortal
wound during his quest, and the sad reality of his departure
was at hand. Approaching the place of their separation, a
tearful Sam spoke.

"But I thought you were going to enjoy the Shire, too, for
years and years, after all you have done."

"So I thought too, once. But I have been too deeply hurt,
Sam. I tried to save the Shire, and it has been saved, but not
for me. It must often be so, Sam, when things are in danger:
some one has to give them up, lose them, so that others may
keep them."

Great sacrifice was necessary to defeat evil. Frodo had been
chosen to carry a load none other could bear and fulfill a task
none other could endure. Though Frodo was only one of
many who had given up something for the greater good,
none had suffered such direct confrontation with darkness or
remained as faithful when tormented by the terrifying, possessing power of wickedness. Such was his role, to lose so
that others might gain. And so, by completing his scene in
the story, Frodo Baggins also performed its most heroic part.

❧ ✝ ❧

Redemption. What a beautiful word! The lost regained. The
ruined restored. The sick healed. The broken repaired. The
enslaved set free. Wrong made right again. The deep yearning
for God finally satisfied by the restoration of goodness!

But redemption can only occur after evil is defeated. Freeing captives requires entering enemy territory. Giving life may
mean facing death. The paradise of peace is often secured
through the hell of war. In every instance, someone must be
willing to give up his or her self for the sake of others. Someone must be a hero.

The essence of every heroic act is self-sacrifice. From the soldier throwing himself onto a live grenade to protect his buddies to an exhausted daughter providing twenty-four-hour care for an ailing parent, heroes are those who give up something for the benefit of others. In the process of giving up themselves, they redeem what is wrong to the right. In a world that has both evil and good, someone must push through the former in order to reclaim the latter.

From soldiers storming the beaches of Normandy to free Europe from tyranny to a frightened hobbit willing to destroy the Ring of Doom, every heroic act is a reflection of the ultimate hero of history, Jesus Christ. He left the respect and comfort of his rightful place for one reason: to redeem you and me from evil. He faced death to give life, endured sorrow to restore joy, confronted hate to show love. He humbled himself to the point of death on a cross to pay for our redemption. He was chosen for a burden none other could bear and a task none other could endure. In his words,

> *God so loved the world that he gave his one and only Son, that whoever believes in him shall not perish but have eternal life. For God did not send his Son into the world to condemn the world, but to save the world through him. (John 3:16-17)*

And in the words of one he redeemed,

> *God demonstrates his own love for us in this: While we were still sinners, Christ died for us. (Romans 5:8)*

And in the words of the jubilant song our story reveals,

You were slain, and with your blood you purchased men
for God from every tribe and language and people and
nation. You have made them to be a kingdom and priests
to serve our God, and they will reign on the earth. . . .
Worthy is the Lamb, who was slain, to receive power and
wealth and wisdom and strength and honor and glory and
praise! (Revelation 5:9-12)

Someday, the rightful King will once again sit on the
throne. All will be as it should be. In a strange twist of
providence, our joy will be greater for having endured sorrow, turning even the intentions of evil into a greater good.
And when that day arrives, the song of all ages will culmi-
nate in a chorus of redemption, a redemption made possible
because the story includes a hero willing to sacrifice himself.
Someone who was, in the words of Frodo, "willing to give
them up, lose them, so that others may keep them."

⬎ *Reflection*
SELF-SACRIFICE IS THE ESSENCE OF EVERY HERO
AND THE ULTIMATE MEANS OF REDEMPTION.

EPILOGUE

It is not difficult to imagine the peculiar
excitement and joy that one would feel
if any specially beautiful fairy-story were
found to be 'primarily' true, its narrative
to be history.

(J. R. R. Tolkien, "On Fairy-stories")

I will shake the nations, and the desired
of all nations will come.

(Haggai 2:7)

Now that this brief tour of Middle-earth is drawing to a
close, it's time for the authors to make a confession: We've
enjoyed it. This attempt at compiling a series of "Christian
reflections" on *The Lord of the Rings* has been, for us, an exer-
cise in pure joy and personal spiritual enrichment.

But this begs a perfectly reasonable question. Enjoyment
is one thing. But what about truth and accuracy? Was it
really fair or true to Tolkien's intent to subject Middle-earth
and its inhabitants to the kind of analysis we've applied?
Is there any justification for wresting from them the mean-
ings and messages this brief volume attempts to convey?

Kurt and I have written from a distinctly Christian point
of view. It's possible that readers who do not appreciate
that perspective will object that we have simply imposed
our own biases and beliefs upon the text of Tolkien's epic.
It's a serious charge, and it deserves a careful answer.

On the other hand, there may be those who share our
Christian convictions but find it impossible to agree that

anything pure, anything holy, anything of true spiritual value can be found in a story that teems with elves, dwarves, goblins, hobbits, wizards, fire demons, and all manner of other strange, imaginary, and magical beings. What do we say to them?

Fortunately, it isn't necessary to say anything that Tolkien hasn't already said himself. He has left us a fairly complete record of his thoughts about questions of this nature. And what he has told us is that fantasy, as he understood it, is, in its highest and purest form, a place where art, theology, and primal human desire meet and intersect. For the Christian this can mean only one thing: Fantasy is a place where we can come face-to-face with Christ.

MAN AS SUB-CREATOR

What was Tolkien's purpose in writing books like *The Silmarillion, The Hobbit,* and *The Lord of the Rings?* In his essay "On Fairy-stories" he gives us a strong clue. Here he defines fantasy as a "Sub-creative Art," the goal of which is to make a "Secondary World" which is marked by "the inner consistency of reality."

"What really happens," he explains, "is that the story-maker proves a successful 'sub-creator.' He makes a Secondary World which your mind can enter. Inside it, what he relates is 'true.' It accords with the laws of that world."[21]

Tolkien, then, was an artist. When he sat down to write, he was trying to make something, something that would be considered beautiful and compelling purely by virtue of its faithfulness to its own inner laws. And it's at this point that the specifically Christian and biblical roots of his thought begin to emerge. As he saw it, "Fantasy is a natural human activity." It's natural because God has made man in his own image (Genesis 1:27). Humans are creators with a small "c"—sub-creators, in Tolkien's terminology—precisely because their Maker is the Creator *par excellence*. Man is possessed of a powerful creative drive, a poignant longing to imitate his great Father in heaven by expressing himself through making.

> *Man, Sub-creator, the refracted Light*
> *through whom is splintered from a single White*
> *to many hues, and endlessly combined*
> *in living shapes that move from mind to mind . . .*
> *'twas our right*
> *(used or misused). That right has not decayed:*
> *we make still by the law in which we're made.*[22]

LEAF BY NIGGLE

Tolkien explored this idea in a short parable or fable entitled *Leaf by Niggle*. Niggle, an insignificant little painter, fritters his life away (or so it seems to everyone else) laboring over a picture of a Great Tree. As he works, his picture grows and expands (much after the fashion of Tolkien's Middle-earth), so that it remains unfinished when the little man is at last called away on his "journey" (that is, when he dies).

Upon reaching paradise, Niggle looks up and is suddenly struck by the oddest, most wondrous realization: He is standing in front of his tree! He is *inside his own painting!* His art has become reality! There he finds his old neighbor, Mr. Parish, and together they employ themselves in caring for the woods, the fields, the hills, and the mountains that had originated in Niggle's imagination. "Niggle would think of wonderful new flowers and plants, and Parish always knew exactly how to set them and where they would do best."[23]

Even so, in Tolkien's vision of things, "[man]. . . may now, perhaps, fairly dare to guess that in Fantasy he may actually assist in the effoliation and multiple enrichment of creation."[24] It is our human destiny to participate with God in the ongoing work of creation.

DESIRE

At the heart of human creativity, says Tolkien, lies desire— "the desire for a living, realized sub-creative art."[25]

Desire. That exquisite, painful longing that is in so many ways the soul of *The Lord of the Rings*. Desire occupies a central place in Tolkien's thinking about the significance of man's subcreative art. In speaking of his own childhood excursions into fantasy and faerie, he writes,

> *At no time can I remember that the enjoyment of a story was dependent on belief that such things could happen, or had happened, in 'real life.' Fairy-stories were plainly not primarily concerned with possibility, but with desirability. If they awakened desire, satisfying it while often whetting it unbearably, they succeeded.*[26]

Something fundamental, he seems to be saying, is missing at the very center of human experience. The best examples of our own creating and making are simply attempts to objectify that something so as to be better able to seek and pursue it. "It's just a story," we say. But in our hearts we know better. The truth is that, at some level too deep for words, we ache for the story to be true.

FAIRY TALE: A TRUE STORY?

Tolkien knew this. "It is not difficult," he wrote, "to imagine the peculiar excitement and joy that one would feel if any specially beautiful fairy-story were found to be 'primarily' true, its narrative to be history."[27]

That thought served as the premise of an intriguing and "specially beautiful" 1997 film, *Fairy Tale: A True Story*.[28] It's the retelling of an actual historical event the way we all *wish* it had happened.

Set in 1917, the film depicts the story of two young girls, Elsie Wright and Frances Griffiths, who become the toast of all England when they not only *see* fairies down by the beck (brook) near Elsie's Yorkshire home, but actually capture their images on film. An expert in photographic trickery vouches for the authenticity of the pictures. What's the world to think? Are there such things as fairies after all?

Two of the period's most noted celebrities become closely involved in the ensuing controversy: writer Sir Arthur Conan Doyle, a spiritualist who enthusiastically endorses the girls' story; and American escape artist Harry Houdini, a savvy illusionist who maintains a ruthlessly cynical attitude toward all reports of supernatural occurrences.

In one particularly poignant scene, after a performance in London Houdini is asked to pose for a picture with Elsie and Frances. There he sits, the great skeptic, an arm around each of the girls, as a reporter asks, "You've seen the Yorkshire photographs. Do you think we're looking at real fairies? I've interviewed you before, Mr. Houdini, and I know you don't stand for any superstitious nonsense."

Houdini's answer might have come straight out of the writings of J. R. R. Tolkien:

> *Sir, I've spent my life making the impossible true. Why*
> *would I find it hard to accept in others? . . . I've stood*
> *against fraud. . . . But I don't see any of that here. I see*
> *only joy.*

Joy. "A fleeting glimpse of Joy," says Tolkien, "Joy beyond
the walls of the world, poignant as grief."[29]

This, as the author of *The Lord of the Rings* saw it, is what
fantasy does best. It gives us a hint, a clue to what we're
really seeking. A "fleeting glimpse of Joy," a painfully tantaliz-
ing taste of ultimate human fulfillment. And this, it seems to
me, is the point of *Fairy Tale: A True Story*. It's all about this
desperate human desire for that poignant, piercing joy.

In the movie version of the story, the desire is gratified.
The fairies turn out to be real. Even Elsie's parents see them
in the final scene. Within the "Secondary World" that the
filmmakers have created, the primal human longing for
"Joy beyond the walls of the world" comes face-to-face with
its object. The distant, beautiful, and indefinable something
we're all wishing for and groping after really does break
through into the mundane reality of workaday existence.

That's what everybody is after, isn't it? That's why Mr.
Houdini never tells people how he "does things." As he
explains it to young Elsie, "No one ever really wants to know
when you do tell them." Of course they don't. What they
want is that the illusion should somehow turn out to be real.

THE BAD NEWS

The bad news is that, in this particular instance, it didn't
turn out to be real. You won't learn this from the movie, but
in actuality, the "true story" of Elsie Wright and Frances
Griffiths did not turn out to have such an exquisitely happy

ending. In real life, both Elsie and Frances confessed as adults that the fairy photos had been a hoax. And when they did, the world breathed a collective sigh of disappointment.

That sigh of disappointment ought to give us pause. It's a reminder of a truth we ignore to our peril. So profound, so powerful, so deeply ingrained in human nature is the desire Tolkien felt when he read fairy-stories as a child that it has the potential to deceive us. It may lead us astray, cause us to jump to conclusions. So badly do we want to believe that we often make an investment of faith and confidence where no such investment is warranted. And when the bottom falls out, when the Elsies and Franceses of the world come clean, we are left with nothing but the dust and ashes of disillusionment.

Is this the end of the line? Is complete skepticism—and beyond that, something even bleaker—our final destiny? The "Fairy Tale" was not "A True Story" after all. Does that mean it's time to turn out the lights and say goodnight?

Some have come to that conclusion. I, for one, cannot. I keep coming back to the existence of the desire itself. Sometimes I forget about it, of course. Sometimes the clutter of everyday life shuts it out. Sometimes boredom, weariness, and the grind of routine dulls its edge. But it never completely goes away. Quietly, subtly, but resolutely, it demands to be heard. Is there nothing "out there" that answers to this nagging, persistent, and apparently universal human craving?

According to Tolkien's friend and colleague C. S. Lewis, there *has* to be. To revisit a statement that was quoted earlier: "Creatures are not born with desires unless satisfaction for those desires exists. A baby feels hunger: well, there is such a thing as food. A duckling wants to swim: well, there is such a thing as water. Men feel sexual desire: well, there is such a thing as sex. If I find in myself a desire which no experience in this world can satisfy, the most probable explanation is that I was made for another world."[30]

THE GOOD NEWS

That's the good news. It's the breathtaking realization that, in a very important sense, our quests are self-validating. It's the inescapable reassurance, rooted in the facts of who and what we are as human beings, that the fairy tale, in all of its excruciating joy, not only *might,* but actually *must,* come true someday.

And what then? What "peculiar excitement and joy" would we feel if the Happy Ending (or, as Tolkien called it, the Eucatastrophe) of the archetypal fairy tale were somehow translated into everyday experience? What if the thing you had always wanted, imagined, dreamed of, projected into your loveliest visions of goodness and beauty but still could never quite put your finger on suddenly leapt into reality and stood there looking at you, large as life, in broad day-light? What if the "piercing beauties" of Tolkien's Middle-earth, for instance, were revealed to be something more than a literary invention? If we, like Niggle, should suddenly find ourselves confronted with the solid reality of our fondest hopes and dreams? What if it all came true?

According to Tolkien, it has.

> *I would venture to say that approaching the Christian Story from this direction, it has long been my feeling (a joyous feeling) that God redeemed the corrupt making-creatures, men, in a way fitting to this aspect, as to others, of their strange nature. The Gospels contain a fairy-story, or a*

> *story of a larger kind which embraces all the essence*
> *of fairy-stories. . . . But this story has entered History*
> *and the primary world; the desire and aspiration of sub-*
> *creation has been raised to the fulfillment of Creation.*[31]

Tolkien was not alone in this belief. One of his contempo-
raries and literary peers, Dorothy Sayers, expressed the
same conviction in the following words:

> *Jesus Christ is unique—unique among gods and men.*
> *There have been incarnate gods a-plenty, and slain-and-*
> *resurrected gods not a few; but He is the only God who*
> *has a date in history.*[32]

C. S. Lewis put it this way:

> *The heart of Christianity is a myth which is also a fact. . . .*
> *It happens—at a particular date, in a particular place,*
> *followed by definable historical consequences. . . . By*
> *becoming fact it does not cease to be myth: that is the*
> *miracle.*[33]

And so we come to the climax. At a particular and forever-
after hallowed point in time, at a small, specific spot on
this tiny globe we call home, the stories all come to life. The
painfully lovely longings embodied in our most cherished
legends leap off the pages and into the light. There in Bethlehem, a door opens in the walls of the world, the veil of
eternity is drawn aside, and the desire of all nations—Jesus
Christ, God in the flesh—steps into our midst.

That, as Tolkien saw it, is *evangelium.*

Good, good news.

Jim Ware

ENDNOTES

1. Humphrey Carpenter, *The Letters of J. R. R. Tolkien* (New York: Houghton Mifflin Company, 2000), 147.
2. J. R. R. Tolkien, *The Tolkien Reader* (New York: Ballantine Books, 1966), 88.
3. Clyde S. Kilby, *Tolkien and The Silmarillion* (Wheaton: Harold Shaw Publishers, 1976), 79.
4. Carpenter, *Letters,* 172.
5. C. S. Lewis, *Mere Christianity* (New York: Touchstone—Simon & Schuster, 1996), 121.
6. J. R. R. Tolkien, *The Silmarillion* (Boston: Houghton Mifflin Company, 1977), 15.
7. Ibid., 16.
8. Ibid., 17-18.
9. J. R. R. Tolkien, *The Hobbit* (New York: Ballantine Books, 1982), 303.
10. *The Dialogues of Plato* (New York: Bantam Books, 1986), 7.
11. Neale Walsch, *Conversations with God* (New York: G.P. Putnam's Sons, 1996), 22.
12. J. R. R. Tolkien, *The Fellowship of the Ring* (New York: Quality Paperback Book Club, 1995), 58.
13. J. R. R. Tolkien, *The Two Towers* (Boston: Houghton Mifflin Company, 1965), 290.
14. Tolkien, *Fellowship*, 93.
15. Malcolm Muggeridge, *The End of Christendom* (Grand Rapids: Wm. B. Ferdmans Publishing Co., 1980), 56.
16. Tolkien, *Silmarillion*, 17.
17. Tolkien, *Towers*, 132.
18. Sir Thomas Malory, *Le Morte d'Arthur* (New York: Penguin Books, 1969), Book XXI, Chapter 7.
19. T. W. Rolleston, *Celtic Myths and Legends* (New York: Dover Publications, 1990), 308. Orginally published as *Myths & Legends of the Celtic Race* (London: George G. Harrap & Company, 1917).
20. Tolkien, *Fellowship,* 394.
21. Tolkien, *Reader*, 37.
22. Ibid., 54.
23. Ibid., 107.
24. Ibid., 73.
25. Ibid., 53.
26. Ibid., 40.
27. Ibid., 72.
28. *Fairy Tale: A True Story.* Directed by Charles Sturridge; written by Albert Ash, Tom McLoughlin, and Ernie Contreras. Paramount Pictures/Icon Productions, 1997.

29. Tolkien, *Reader*, 68.
30. Lewis, *Mere Christianity*, 121.
31. Tolkien, *Reader*, 71-72.
32. Dorothy L. Sayers, *The Man Born to Be King* (London: Victor Gollancz LTD, 1943), 20.
33. C. S. Lewis, *God in the Dock* (Grand Rapids: Wm. B. Eerdmans Publishing Co., 1970), 66-67.

ABOUT THE AUTHORS

Kurt Bruner is a vice president with Focus on the Family, where he leads in the creation of books, films, magazines, and radio drama, including the popular Adventures in Odyssey series and the Peabody Award-winning Focus on the Family Radio Theatre programs. The author of several books, including The Divine Drama, Kurt lives in Colorado Springs, Colorado, with his wife and four halflings.

Freelance writer Jim Ware is a graduate of Fuller Theological Seminary and the author of several books. He became a Tolkien fan during his freshman year of high school during the 1960s. Jim lives in Colorado Springs with his wife and six children. He wears one ring.

THE DIVINE DRAMA

Good stories express what we already know deep within us—tapping into our highest hopes and deepest longings, transforming our minds and hearts. Within the pages of *The Divine Drama*, author Kurt Bruner shares his powerful encounter with the most captivating story of all—God's story. In this three-part book, Bruner beautifully recounts God's story as an epic drama, leading you to a discovery of your own place on God's stage—and giving you tools for living out that role on a daily basis. Experience the awe and wonder of the story above all stories—and discover the significance of the part you play in God's drama.